D0428727

Praise for
22 Keys to Sales Success:
How to Make It Big in Financial Services
by James M. Benson and Paul Karasik

"Jim Benson and Paul Karasik have written an easy-to-read-and-understand, jam-packed guide to proven successful selling techniques. I would categorize this book as a must-read for new sales professionals and a you-better-read for seasoned sales professionals."

ALBERT J. "BUD" SCHIFF
CEO, NYLEX Benefits
Past President, Association for Advanced Life Underwriting (AALU)
Past Chairman, International Top of the Table

"This is one of the best-written sales books I've seen. The action steps and skill builders help put words into action. This belongs on the shelf of every sales professional in the financial services business."

ROBERT B. PLYBON
Plybon & Associates
Past President, Million Dollar Round Table

"22 Keys to Sales Success makes a great educational text for the financial professional. It presents new ideas for the experienced adviser while also reinforcing historical best practices. For the less-experienced adviser, it serves as an effective primer on how to build a successful practice. Don't miss the resources guide in the back of the book—that alone is worth the price of admission!"

BARRY G. KNIGHT
President, NEXT Financial Group

"With this book, Jim Benson and Paul Karasik share their expertise on a number of important skills—such as developing client and professional relationships; ascertaining and serving client needs; and formulating, implementing, and adjusting multifaceted plans—in a clear, articulate, and practical way. *22 Keys to Sales Success* **provides the next generation of producers and leaders the tools they need to be successful in this ever-changing industry.**"

DAVID STERTZER
Executive Vice President, Association for Advanced Life Underwriting

"Benson and Karasik are prophets when it comes to increasing your profits. *22 Keys* **will unlock hundreds of doors, leading you to thousands of people who can make you millions of dollars.** Superb! A must-read for people who must succeed!"

JOEY REIMAN
Thinker & CEO, BrightHouse, LLC

"**Much more than a sales how-to,** *22 Keys* **can help unlock your potential for success.** A commonsense approach to increasing your business."

RANDALL JONES
Financial Services Adviser
Major wirehouse, Princeton, New Jersey

22 KEYS TO SALES SUCCESS

22 KEYS TO SALES SUCCESS

How to Make It Big in
Financial Services

James M. Benson
Paul Karasik

BLOOMBERG PRESS

NEW YORK

This publication contains the authors' opinions and is designed to provide accurate and authoritative information. It is sold with the understanding that the authors, publisher, and Bloomberg L.P. are not engaged in rendering legal, accounting, investment-planning, or other professional advice. The reader should seek the services of a qualified professional for such advice; the authors, publisher, and Bloomberg L.P. cannot be held responsible for any loss incurred as a result of specific investments or planning decisions made by the reader.

Note: For guidance in matters of compliance, please refer to the rules and regulations of the agencies that govern the products and services associated with your practice. The strategies and techniques presented in this book should not be interpreted as providing such guidance.

First edition published 2004
5 7 9 10 8 6

ISBN-13: 978-1-57660-149-5

The Library of Congress has cataloged the earlier printing as follows:

Benson, James M.
    22 keys to sales success: how to make it big in financial services / James M. Benson, Paul Karasik.
        p. cm.
Includes bibliographical references.
    ISBN 1-57660-149-8 (alk. paper)
    1. Cross-selling financial services. 2. Relationship banking. 3. Brokers--Vocational guidance. I. Title: Twenty-two keys to sales success. II. Title.

HG1616 . M3B44 2004
332.1 ' 068 ' 8--dc22   2003028159

Acquired and edited by Kathleen A. Peterson

To the thousands of World T.E.A.M. Sports athletes,
who have participated in extraordinary feats of endurance,
camaraderie, and fortitude. In acknowledgment of their dynamic
spirit and initiative, 100 percent of my portion of this
book's royalties will be donated to World T.E.A.M. Sports.

Jim Benson

To the old schoolmaster, Nat Karasik
and to my inspiration, Samantha

Paul Karasik

CONTENTS

Preface

THE GENESIS AND MOTIVATION FOR WRITING THIS BOOK ARE reflected within the meaning of the following story.

A man is on his hands and knees under a street light late one evening. Another man comes along and realizes that he is upset and searching for something. He stops to help and asks, "What are you looking for?"

The man on the ground replies, "The keys to my house."

The man who was out for an evening walk decides to help. He joins the man down on the ground and begins to assist him in the search for the keys.

After a while he asks, "Do you have any idea where you lost them?"

The man says, "Up there by the front door to my house."

The man trying to help is bewildered and asks, "So why are you looking for them down here?"

The searching man looks up and replies, "Because the light is a lot better down here."

This book originated almost ten years ago. Much of the initial content evolved in conversations my coauthor Jim Benson and I had "on the run." Well, actually, during a series of very long runs. Jim and I regularly pounded out twenty-mile training runs circling the island of Manhattan, during which we shared our thoughts, ideas, and feelings on things we both were passionate about. One of the topics we shared then, and continue to share much enthusiasm about, is selling. Jim and I hold some common and some unique perspectives on selling financial products and services.

Jim began his career with a dream and a personal vision of success that far exceeded that of the average producer. He saw the financial industry as the arena in which to go exponentially further than making a good living while simultaneously making a positive contribution to society. Jim recognized selling as the door to manifesting his dreams, maximizing his potential, and achieving unlimited success.

As a producer Jim dedicated himself to mastering the art and science of sales and marketing. He understood the value of sales training and embraced the underlying concepts that the top producers lived by. And along the way Jim developed his own set of strategies and techniques. Within a relatively few years Jim's personal production ranked with the best of the best in the financial industry.

Based upon his monumental sales success, Jim gained recognition and earned his most recent positions, which have included holding top executive positions at three of the largest and most prestigious financial organizations in the world. Currently, as the leader of literally thousands of industry producers, Jim continues to monitor and encourage others to seize the opportunity.

My initial perception of selling was shaped by my father, who was a salesman for the better part of his life. In fact, at eighty-three, on his way to a closing of a sale, he pulled his car over and died peacefully doing what he loved. I remember him telling me, when as a troubled and concerned fifteen year old I pondered what my career path might be, "Son, learn how to sell and you will never have to worry about making a living."

He would talk to me about selling from the "old school" perspective. Some of the methods are not applicable in today's marketplace (and frankly, probably should not have been practiced back then, either). But a lot of the concepts my dad spoke to me about are the foundation upon which all great salespeople build their careers, regardless of whether they are selling life insurance or life preservers.

While still young, I struggled to make a transition in my life away from an uneven lifestyle as a songwriter and musician. It was at that point the seeds my father planted began to take root. I dedicated my professional life to selling and eventually became a sales and management consultant in the financial industry. As a consultant I continue to capture and systematize the best practices of those who have achieved greatness in the industry.

Each year the financial services industry attracts thousands of individuals hungry for the rewards the industry offers both on the material as well as the internal level. Unfortunately, the vast majority, about 90 percent, will fail within five years. Not because the industry is exclusive to a particular type of person. In fact, anyone, regardless of social background, sex, race, or religion, has a truly equal opportunity to make more money than in almost any other career track.

Most people will fail because they are like the misguided soul in the opening story. They are searching in vain for the keys in the wrong place. If you want to open the door to success, this book is the right place.

Perhaps the format of this book was influenced by the short, rhythmic, and measured placement of our feet along the urban trails when the content of this book initially began to surface. Or perhaps the format of this book arose from the love both Jim and I have for music in all of its myriad manifestations.

From Beethoven to the Beatles, from James Brown to Johnny Cash, the power and majesty of all music to raise our spirits and touch our souls is derived from the same twelve tones. Likewise every salesperson is given a limited set of notes to play. In this book each of these notes is represented as a key to success.

It is up to you to arrange and apply each of these keys in your own way and in your own style to create your own success. Both Jim and I are confident these keys will provide a path for anyone who is seeking to open the door to unlimited success in selling financial products and services. After reading this book you will have the keys; the only question is, will you choose to open the door?

PAUL KARASIK

Introduction

I F YOU WANT TO MAKE MORE MONEY, HAVE MORE FUN, WORK less, and get more satisfaction from your work, this book is for you. It is a road map for the licensed financial professional who has recently entered the business as well as a resource for the experienced professional who is seeking to achieve higher levels of success.

The financial industry has undergone dynamic structural change in the past few years. These changes have deeply affected financial products, distribution systems, and the way financial products and services are sold. Today's financial marketplace demands a more savvy and informed sales and marketing approach.

Many of the high-pressure, product-oriented sales and marketing strategies and techniques that worked in the past are no longer applicable in today's market. In the past, selling was product centered. People today typically already have access to unlimited product information, creating confusion for the consumer and a need for new approaches for the financial professional. Today, establishing trust and building relationships with clients have become not only a priority but a necessity for long-term marketing success.

Changes in the distribution of financial products and services have also created a demand for the information in this book. The insurance industry, for one, has largely transitioned from a captive sales force approach to an independent system of specialists representing the products of many companies. Equally profound, aside from the few remaining large insurance companies, most insurance professionals have little opportunity for sales and marketing training. Thus, also, the need for this book.

Investment professionals also are receiving less sales training. In an effort to reduce expenses, large brokerage firms have cut back dramatically on sales training. The significant rise in the number of independent financial advisers, by definition, makes providing for their professional development more complex.

Thus, the audience for this book spans an incredible variety of professional settings, business models, and products and services. The book addresses individuals selling primarily one type of product or service, independent professionals who sell many different products and services, professionals who earn commissions, and those who earn fees.

22 Keys to Sales Success: How to Make It Big in Financial Services is directed to those working for large companies, those who work out of home offices, those working in banks, and those who are on the road and rarely see the inside of any office. This book is for individuals with a wide range of professional designations and professional titles, including, but not limited to, CFP, CLU, LUTCF, RIA, FIC, ChFC, CFS, CSA, CRPC, CPA, CCPS, J.D., and M.B.A.

Because the audience for this book is so varied, we have used the term financial professional throughout for the sake of simplicity in writing. The reader is reminded that the book is a resource for the new and experienced professional, and for those selling a variety of financial products and services, whether attached to a company or independent. In an effort to address the diversity of our audience, we have used a variety of examples specific to certain industry subgroups.

But the unique thread that binds you all as the audience for this book is the importance of your work: to help people manage their financial lives more wisely and successfully. This outcome in turn helps clients to feel more secure and enjoy their lives more fully with less worry about financial soundness. It doesn't matter if your products are directed toward wealth accumulation, preservation, or transfer. The thread that binds you cannot be dismissed as insignificant. You are the in the Quality of Life business.

You are selling products and services that in many cases play a major role in people's lives. Your role might be protecting families and assets with risk management products, advising clients on investment products that help to create rich and well-deserved retirements, creating plans that generate meaningful social legacies that make the world a better place, or whatever goal your client has in mind.

It is simple to say that you are not selling golf clubs or washing machines. What you do is very important in the lives of your clients. The intention of this book is single-minded: to help you to achieve your short- and long-term goals in this business. Because what you do is important.

This book is written to be read, internalized, and acted upon. It is rich with both strategy and technique. The concepts and ideas are both sophisticated and practical at the same time. The tone is both weighty and lighthearted. You will want to learn from this book, but you will also enjoy the process. Some of the Keys will take months to implement and can take a lifetime to perfect. Others you can implement in an hour and benefit from for an entire career.

The 22 Keys represent a combination of our own personal experience in sales and marketing and the ageless wisdom of the masters in the financial products and services industry. Even though the industry and the products and services will continue to change, we believe the underlying principles we refer to as Keys will remain the foundation for success for decades to come.

Most of the Keys are specific to the financial industry, while others are founded on an understanding of the nature of human behavior and psychology. To be successful you must become enlightened in both areas of expertise.

We hope this book becomes the definitive statement for maximizing your sales potential in the financial industry. But we also understand and appreciate the need for an ongoing investment in your professional development. Each Key in this book unlocks a door to your future. Go through one door, and you will find many other doors for you to explore in depth and apply to your business practices.

When you are ready to open new doors to professional development, there are lots of other things you can do to follow. Go to sales seminars, enroll in formal training sessions, seek out mentors, hire coaches, continue to read personal and professional development books, become active in trade and professional organizations. Learn what you need to be a modern practitioner. In addition, by helping others who are less experienced than you, you'll gain fresh insights on your own abilities and perhaps see where you have become complacent or need to sharpen your skills.

Yes, this book will fill your bucket with knowledge, but ultimately we also want to light a fire. The 22 Keys to Sales Success are meant to inspire you to go beyond your current level of accomplishment. If you never stop growing, always seeking improvement, it's the ultimate key to success in career and life.

KEY 1

Take Control of the Sale

If you don't sell, it's not the product that's wrong, it's you.

—ESTÉE LAUDER

THERE ARE NO PROFESSIONAL PROSPECTS. THERE *ARE* PROFES-
sional salespeople. It's up to you to take control of the selling
process and guide the prospect through the sale to its conclusion. If
you give up control, by letting your prospect dominate the sales presentation, you are letting an amateur take over. The first key to selling is to always maintain control of the sales process and to monitor
the prospective client's reactions and responses, as well as manage
any obstructing behavior, all along the way.

The prospective buyer is not trained to know the twenty-five best
questions to ask a financial professional. Remaining conscious of
this will eliminate your frustration if and when the sales presentation
wanders and will endow you with the patience you need when the
prospect gets off track. You need to be part psychologist as you work
with your potential clients to move them through the sales cycle. The
psychological aspect of the sales process is to anticipate the reactions of the prospect and be prepared with solutions that will keep
the selling discussion headed in the right direction.

You must understand the prospect's mind-set. If you don't understand and address the prospective client's mind-set, you will find that successful selling becomes difficult, if not impossible. Most people spend the better part of each day thinking about themselves: their worries, their goals, their daily tasks. During the sales discussion the mind of every prospect is preoccupied with the two Big Questions:

1. What's in it for me?
2. Do I trust this person?

From the moment of contact, the single most important objective you have is to provide both logical *and* emotional answers to the Big Questions. Relationship building and the sales process will progress as long as you continue to answer these Big Questions. Thus in any sales discussion it's essential that you always anticipate the prospect's concern for the personal payoff. Trust is a more elusive goal to achieve. The best way to approach this Big Question is to present your capabilities as well as pointing out where you *can't* help the prospect, to continuously ask the buyer if he or she has any questions, and to offer reassurance through frequent references to past experiences involving similar issues and solutions.

Although there is no one sales personality, salespeople share one common trait: selling is always ego-driven; it involves a strong desire to take control. The glaring paradox is that successful selling requires the salesperson to make personal ego secondary to the prospect's needs.

Selling is not the place to get *your* needs met. It is the place for you to meet the needs of your potential client and for you to then go to the bank with the results. So control your ego's desire for conquest and defer to the prospect. Remember, the ultimate goal is to make the buyer comfortable—to put him in a mind-set to trust you and then to buy!

It would be nice to believe that human beings purchase financial products and services based purely on information and logic—that is, the features and benefits of the product they are considering buying, its economic value, and its relevance to their financial circumstances. Although you cannot make a financial sale without providing these details, your success in closing the sale will be determined not by the logic of your presentation but rather by your ability to control your prospect's emotions. These emotions can be difficult to detect, bring to the surface, and resolve. Fear is the predominant emotion you must learn to detect and control, although the prospect will rarely disclose it as such. It is your responsibility to uncover, understand, and allay the various fears that drive your prospect to indecision and threaten to destroy your sale.

How can you tell when fear is holding back your prospect? If she is stalling by asking extraneous questions or otherwise not choosing to move ahead with a decision, you can safely assume fear is part of the problem. Fear is also displayed physically, so be alert to body language. Signals of fear include crossed arms or busy hands, a leaning-away posture, grimaces or pained facial expressions, and the failure to stand or sit face-to-face with you. If you observe such signals, you need to address the prospect's fear before you can move ahead. Below are the four primary fears that threaten to destroy your sale and suggestions for helping your prospects overcome them.

1. Fear of making the wrong decision. The buyer of financial products is continually being offered conflicting advice by financial gurus on the radio and television. Ads for financial products and services pelt consumers everywhere they turn. Telemarketers call relentlessly with investment opportunities. The buyer is overwhelmed by myriad products and services from which to choose. Uncertain and volatile financial markets erode confidence in the financial products and services you offer. It is no surprise the consumer is confused, indecisive, and even terrified.

The solution. The financial professional must assume the role of an educator. Your intention is not to make your prospects experts in financial planning, insurance, or investments. Rather, you must interview your prospects, gather information about their goals and knowledge, and then, based on this information, carefully explain how a particular investment opportunity or financial product will meet their needs. Don't teach them how to make a decision, but do teach them why they should do so. The best way to control this aspect of fear is to support your claims with simple, neutral, factual information, such as newspaper articles, investment service reports (ValueLine, for example), and charts that show investment performance against a well-known index (such as the S&P 500). By providing factual information for the buyer to use in making a decision, you highlight your role as an educator and downplay your image as a salesman.

2. Fear of change. The buyer knows that any financial decision is a step away from the status quo: that is, what is comfortable. Change of any kind is disturbing. The fear associated with taking action, often into unknown areas, can keep a buyer frozen in place. This fear is amplified when your potential client is presented with the prospect of a major decision and lacks experience with the product or service you are offering. For example, someone who has never purchased insurance will fear buying it more than someone who has bought it in the past. Such fear is a powerful inhibitor of the sales process and yet, as has been noted, may be hard to detect because it is so easily disguised.

The solution. Provide prospects with a road map for the decision making process. Let them know what to expect. It's like a trip to the dentist. If the dentist said you had a problem and immediately began injecting, poking, scraping, and drilling in your mouth with big chrome instruments, your fear level would be 100 percent. On the other hand, if the dentist first took X-rays, showed you a model of the tooth or a videotape of the procedure, and carefully explained what to expect during each step, your fear level would be much lower. Information is the greatest antidote to fear.

In a similar fashion, the prospect needs a plan of the selling process and what will take place. This plan could include information such as the length and content of the fact-finding interview, where it will take place (a comfortable location), the agenda of follow-up meetings, and how each of you will decide if the relationship is a fit. These steps are critically important to establishing credibility and trust with the prospective client, and describing them is the best way to handle fear of change.

3. Fear of giving up control. Buyers walk into any selling situation with the need to feel in control. They want to establish the ground rules, direct the process, and feel they have the ultimate power over the seller. Fear of giving up this control is reflected in a variety of behaviors. The prospect may not return phone calls or may delay returning them. Sometimes the prospect may force you to set appointments with little regard for your schedule. He may reschedule or cancel appointments, disregarding the inconvenience to you. Or he may stall or delay the process, calling you back several times before making a final decision.

In addition, the buyer may demonstrate fear of giving up control by asking impossible questions that are intended to reveal lack of expertise on your part. Psychologically, these actions give the buyer the feeling of having the upper hand. The problem is that such behavior is counterproductive to a mutually trustworthy relationship and ultimately to a sale.

The solution. The secret to overcoming your prospect's fear of giving up control is to ask for permission and agreement. Ask for permission to question. Ask for agreement on how you will set and keep appointments. Ask for an agreement that each of you will keep your word. Ask for agreement on how to proceed with each step of the sales discussion. By asking for agreement and permission, you reduce, and hopefully avoid, the obstacles that can be created by the fear of giving up control. These tactics allow you to manage the selling process while giving the buyer equity in the relationship so that he remains comfortable.

4. Fear of losing self-esteem. Many people who are self-assured in other areas feel quite inadequate when discussing financial products and services. People have emotional and ego attachments to money. When their egos are at stake (they may truly feel incompetent to manage their financial affairs), their self-esteem is threatened.

Making a purchase decision intensifies this fear, because poor financial choices threaten self-esteem. At a cocktail party, some people are quick to share the incredible returns of a successful investment, but most people are a little shy about discussing the investment pick that failed. Lack of expertise and insufficient knowledge about your products and services will also contribute to a potential client's feelings of inadequacy. A perceived threat to your potential client's self-esteem is probably the most serious emotional factor you will encounter. It initiates the strongest defense mechanisms and derails your sales presentation.

The solution. There are two parts here. First, always do the right thing. Always sell the right product to the right person at the right time. Second, always communicate in a way that makes your prospects feel good about themselves. How and what you say must communicate concern, respect, and patience. Make your prospects feel good about doing business with you: they made the right choice.

—‖—

The first key to success in selling financial products and services is to maintain influence over your potential client's state of mind. If the sales process does not go the way you would like it to, it is probably because you have relinquished control or the prospective client's fear has taken over. You are the professional in this relationship. You must lead and control every aspect of the sales process. Give up control and allow your prospect's fear to creep in, and you give up the sale. Be acutely aware of the emotional reactions of your prospective client to the sales presentation. The four fears can ruin a sales discussion by creating undisclosed mistrust and lack of confidence in the potential transaction. Be on the lookout for signs of hesitation by the potential client. They reveal a fear that you will need to address to keep the sales process on target.

▶▶ *ACTION STEP*

USE POWER PHRASES

Start using the following power phrases to take control when you are selling. Adapt and modify them to fit your selling style and your buyer's demeanor. They will help you take control and defuse the unspoken fears that can destroy a sale.

>> "The truth is that if you weren't feeling a little uncomfortable about making a big decision, I'd wonder about the seriousness of your intentions."

>> "I know how you feel. A lot of people have felt the same way. What I have found helpful is ..."

>> "What you are feeling is quite normal. It makes a lot of sense to me. Here are some things to think about: ... "

>> "From my experience, your concerns are quite typical. Most of my clients ..."

>> "What do you need to know to make you comfortable with ...?"

>> "Don't worry about understanding this immediately. It usually takes a little while for most people to grasp ... "

>> "That's an excellent question! Many of my clients have asked the same thing."

>> "Let's use this meeting to create a plan on how we can move forward. Does that make sense to you?"

>> "Probably the best way to find out if we are a fit is for me to ask you some questions and for you to ask me about anything you need to know. Does that sound right?"

>> "If it weren't for this issue, would there be any other reason you wouldn't start this program today, or begin the transfer process?"

>> "Can you see how this program will help you meet your goals? If you won't do it with me, will you at least promise you'll do it with somebody? (Big trust builder.)

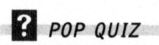

POP QUIZ

Which of the following roles reflect professionalism in the sales process?

a. Consultant e. Antagonist
b. Educator f. Coach
c. Doormat g. Hockey puck
d. Psychologist

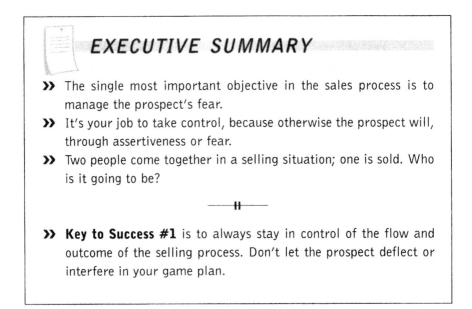

EXECUTIVE SUMMARY

» The single most important objective in the sales process is to manage the prospect's fear.

» It's your job to take control, because otherwise the prospect will, through assertiveness or fear.

» Two people come together in a selling situation; one is sold. Who is it going to be?

———‖———

» **Key to Success #1** is to always stay in control of the flow and outcome of the selling process. Don't let the prospect deflect or interfere in your game plan.

KEY 2

Focus on Clients, Not Compensation

If you want to win the game of selling
keep your eye on the ball, not the scoreboard.

—ANONYMOUS

VERY FEW PEOPLE GO TO COLLEGE THINKING, "AH, ONE DAY I'm going to sell financial products and services." Yet each year, attracted by the benefits of a career in the financial industry, tens of thousands of people get licensed and enter the business.

Unfortunately, the vast majority of newcomers to the business leave it in a matter of months. And sadly, many of those who generate enough sales to stay in the business fail to achieve anywhere near their potential because they have made a critical mistake in their focus. They are more attuned to the rewards than to the clients.

The secret to long-term, unlimited success in the financial products and services business is to focus on clients, not commissions or fees. A client is defined as someone who has bought products or services from you in the past, is willing and able to continue buying from you in the future, and can refer you to other potential clients.

The terms *client* and *customer* are used carefully here. A client is a person, as suggested above, with whom you build a trusting, long-term, personal and professional relationship that results in repeat business. A customer, on the other hand, is someone who buys one product or service from you and has no further perceived needs to be developed. Both are important sources of income, but having a select group of *clients* is the ultimate goal. To create a thriving practice, you need only one specific target: to add one client—not one customer—to your business each week.

Early on, the distinction between client and customer is not too clear. Generally, a client will be looking for a financial adviser, and a customer will be looking for an economical salesperson. Medium term, the client has bought into the framework for a financial plan that you have laid out and is beginning to buy the products you recommend to fit that plan, whereas the customer has probably not called you back looking for second-tier products and services, even though you have made the effort to communicate.

Longer term, clients develop complete trust in your ability to help them plan their financial future and to provide quality products and services for their financial needs. Over the medium to long term—say, five years—clients are your main source of referrals and new business. A financial specialist who has 200 customers spends 80 percent of his time prospecting for new business. A financial specialist who has 200 clients spends 20 percent of his time prospecting for new business. The difference is clear.

—H—

Virtually everyone who enters the financial services industry is entrepreneurial. You get into this field to be an independent businessperson, to help people secure a financial future, and to make lots of money. The financial industry offers you the freedom to create a business that is suited to your personality, to the products and services you want to sell, and to your target market. You also want to get paid what you feel you are worth, not what someone else has decided you are worth. Money is one of the primary motivations for entering this industry, and that's a good thing, but it should not be your primary focus. Managing and developing your client base is the precursor to making money.

Three selling skills are required to implement this key and to establish a client, rather than a customer, base. The first is *focus*. In most cases, it will take more energy to qualify and develop a client than it does to get a customer. But if your focus is clear, you are much more likely to achieve your goal. Therefore, concentrate on developing clients at the beginning of your career and you will be laying the groundwork for a practice built on clients instead of customers.

The second skill you need is the *discipline* to *stay* focused on what you want. Knowing that clients are exceedingly more valuable than customers does not always transfer into action. This is especially true if you fail to do the right thing when faced with the opportunity to grab the "short money." Your long-term success will be determined by your discipline—the discipline to reject customers if they are taking too much time and resources away from servicing your clients.

The third, and most difficult, selling skill is *patience*. Even with focus and discipline, it is not always easy to know in the early stages of a relationship who will be a customer and who will be a client. Unfortunately, as mentioned previously, there is no quick answer or litmus test. Some prospects who you initially believed would be merely customers may turn out to be clients, and vice versa. You will need to employ patience and allow the relationship to unfold. Allow yourself time to confirm that you have chosen a client. Eventually, if no repeat business or referrals result from the relationship, you will see that you have a customer, not a client. You then need to decide how much energy to put into this customer, if any.

Again, the important lesson to take from all of this is to avoid the trap of placing too much importance on how much money you make in the short run, and to concentrate instead on how many client relationships you are creating. *The client-focused practice is orientated toward long-term, profitable relationships.* Customer and client relationships both provide sales. Both require about the same amount of effort. But over time, the client relationship will be exponentially more profitable, because of repeat and referral business.

Customer-Focused Practice   **Client-Focused Practice**

The accompanying illustration demonstrates the underlying truth of this principle. In the first five years, no matter how well you do, the amount of money you make is insignificant compared with what you can make in the second or third five-year interval—assuming you expend your efforts on securing and growing clients. If you do that, you will maximize your potential and create the wealth the financial services business has to offer. The simple mathematical rule at work here is compounded interest. Just like a bank account, a quality client "compounds" by buying more products and services from you over time and creating referrals.

Your goal over the next three or four years should be to develop relationships with about 200 people who qualify as clients. These are people who rely on you, and you, likewise, rely on them. That's the basis for building a business. If you continue to strive toward this objective, you're in the business. If you don't, you're out of it, or you probably should be, based on low income alone.

By its nature—that of building long-term, trusting relationships with clients—this is one of the toughest businesses to get into. Because of competition from other entrepreneurs and financial institutions, it's hard to find clients who aren't already "taken." But with 200 clients, it's almost impossible to get out of the business. This is the core clientele you need to guarantee repeat business and leave enough time for prospecting.

Client-focused practices experience an accelerated liftoff. The first few years are moderately successful, but in the succeeding years growth is exponential—compounded, as mentioned earlier. The illustration below demonstrates this phenomenon.

Most financial professionals fail to achieve their income potential because they do not discriminate between clients and customers. Running a financial products and services business based on customers alone is exhausting. Every day you must devote a significant part of your time to prospecting, since customers are one- or two-sale buyers. Customers have no loyalty because there is no relationship. They buy financial products and services from the lowest bidder, from a "specialty" referral (an insurance agent, for example), or simply from a name out of the yellow pages. Customers are more interested in price because they take the short-term view and do not value an ongoing relationship with a financial products and services provider. You tend to spend the same up-front time with a customer or a client, but the rewards are smaller and short term with a customer. For these reasons, businesses based on customers are extremely hard work with minimal repeat business.

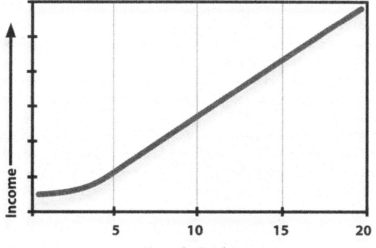

Years in Business

Clients, on the other hand, have a different psychology. First, they are looking to coordinate all their financial needs with one provider. They are looking to build a relationship with one adviser rather than with an insurance agent, a broker, a retirement planner, and other specialized providers. Clients want their needs to be understood by a single trusted and established professional. Naturally, it can take longer to develop these relationships, as shown in the previous illustration. But the long-term benefit of having a client base far outweighs the benefit of just having customers.

Clients can start with simple insurance solutions, migrate into retirement or education planning, and end up with a complete portfolio of products and services from one provider: you. As the relationship grows, less maintenance work is required, because of the knowledge, trust, and loyalty developed over the years. You are the first person a client calls when he needs help. Client relationships need to be cultivated and massaged, of course, but that's far less work than chasing down new customers every day.

—‖—

Accepting short-term business drains resources and time that you could be using to prospect and service clients. Maintaining a client focus requires discipline, patience, and determination, but the long-term benefits make the effort worthwhile. Therefore, each day you must aim to establish serious, sincere, business-oriented relationships. You will make much more than a living when you create these long-term relationships with clients; you'll make a life and a successful career.

A word about commissions and fees. If you are already in business and have decided to charge your clients commissions on what you sell them, then fine. But for those of you who have some flexibility, consider a fee-based compensation arrangement based on the professional advice you provide *in addition* to commissions on products. You may begin a relationship with a customer who you think will become a client with a commission-based system. But make it clear that when the relationship evolves into investment *advice and planning,* your compensation will include a fee. The fee you charge can be structured in many ways, but the most common model is a percentage of the gross gain in the client's portfolio value over a period of time. When you charge a fee, the client is guaranteed that you will put the work into your recommendations and that both of you will benefit from your expertise as the value of the assets increases.

▶▶ ACTION STEP 1

APPLY THE PARETO PRINCIPLE

One powerful concept for improving your sales and marketing efforts is the Pareto Principle, or the Law of 80/20. In 1906, Italian economist Vilfredo Pareto described the economic distribution of wealth as a mathematical formula: 80 percent of the wealth, he said, is held by 20 percent of the population.

After Pareto made his observation, many others observed similar phenomena in their own areas of expertise. Today, the Pareto Principle provides valuable guidance and direction in many areas of sales and marketing.

Using the Pareto Principle, in the early years of your practice you may find that 80 percent of the people you do business with are customers, and the other 20 percent are clients. But more important, you'll find that 80 percent of your income is being produced by those 20 percent who qualify as clients. With that in mind, you can do a simple exercise to increase your income. Review each customer in the 80 percent segment one by one, and evaluate the potential of each to become a client. Pursue repeat and referral business with those who you believe could become clients. Spend your time and attention on transitioning these people from customer to client relationships.

POP QUIZ

Use the immutable Pareto Principle to answer these questions.

1. *How much would your income increase if 80 percent of the people with whom you do business were clients rather than customers?*
   a. 80 percent
   b. 100 percent
   c. 250 percent (correct answer)
2. *If you have eighty customers and twenty clients, how many new client relationships do you need to double your business?*
   a. one hundred
   b. fifty
   c. twenty-five (correct answer)

▶▶ ACTION STEP 2

REMAIN CLIENT-FOCUSED

1. Stop wasting time with obvious customer relationships. Focus on people who come to you for broad financial advice or who you think could benefit from your expertise.
2. Get one new customer each week who qualifies as a potential client.
3. Visualize five new client relationships a month. You will need this productivity to get to 200 to 300 clients in five years.
4. Now go out and do it. (Don't forget to fasten your seat belt!)

EXECUTIVE SUMMARY

>> Successful businesses are based on lasting, growing client relationships.

>> While customers are an easier sell, they tend to be "shoppers."

>> Clients may take longer to cultivate, but their ROI is far greater.

>> Businesses based on client relationships start out on a flatter sales curve, but after about five years the curve accelerates.

>> Short-term-thinking entrepreneurs should consider a business other than selling financial products and services.

>> A successful client-oriented business can be built on 200 to 300 clients acquired over five years. These clients are your referral source, allowing you to spend 80 percent of your time cultivating them and 20 percent of your time prospecting for new clients.

---||---

>> **Key to Success #2** is choosing the right mix of customers and clients as your practice grows. Customers are for today; clients are forever.

KEY **3**

Position with Mission

The first principle of ethical power is purpose....
By purpose, we mean your objective or intention—something
toward which you are always striving. Purpose is something bigger.
It is the picture you have of yourself—the kind of person
you want to be or the kind of life you want to lead.

—KENNETH BLANCHARD AND NORMAN VINCENT PEALE

THE ADEPT FINANCIAL PRODUCTS AND SERVICES PROVIDER has a positioning mission. Why? Because too often the consumer is confused. Easy access and the similarity of financial products and services have leveled the playing field. Not only have all of the products and services begun to look alike, but so have the people offering them. The market for financial products and services has been commoditized.

For the consumer, buying financial products and services is a lot like buying water. If you want to put yourself in your prospect's shoes, go to the beverage aisle of your local supermarket. Assuming the price of each is about the same, how do you decide which brand of water is the right one for you? Each bottle comes from purported pure crystalline springs in a variety of attractive locales, such as Alaska, Hawaii, Idaho, Montana, Washington, Vermont, and the like. From the consumer's perspective, they all look alike. They all look like water. That's why consumers have a real problem making a decision.

Look at the advertisements for financial services companies and products long enough, and you'll see that they begin to blur and blend into one another. All the investment and insurance companies want to be your trusted adviser, your friend, the best company you keep, your most secure relationship, and so on. The financial consumer experiences the same confusion you did when shopping for water. As you can see, distributors of bottled water face a problem creating a competitive advantage in the marketplace. You have a similar problem, but fortunately you can address it more easily.

The secret to competitive advantage resides in the ability to uniquely position your products and services. Positioning refers to how differently your prospect perceives your business. Therefore, good positioning is not about your products; it's about managing the way you are perceived. It is a method to allow you and your financial products and services to stand out in an overcrowded marketplace. Positioning, or differentiation, provides you with a competitive advantage. In addition to that strong incentive, here are six more good reasons to tightly position your business.

1. **Your organization will become more efficient** because you will design sales approaches and solutions that you can use again and again.
2. **You will become an expert with a specific group** and therefore more credible and attractive to this set of prospects.
3. **Your marketing plan will be easier to design** because it will be targeted.
4. **You will become more efficient at qualifying prospects** because your positioning (targeting) will limit the number of people who respond to you.
5. **Referrals will increase** because you will generate word of mouth about your specialty.
6. **You will enjoy working with your clients more** because they are people you have chosen and with whom you have a natural rapport.

Your Mission Statement

If you want to position your practice, you must create a mission-driven organization. This means you must become clear on what you do, why you do it, and for whom you do it. You can communicate your position with a mission statement. Your mission statement will describe the compelling reasons a certain group of prospects should do business with you rather than with other providers. Your mission, or purpose, will act as a magnet for attracting more clients and fewer customers.

Besides positioning you, your purpose will add meaning to your day-to-day work experience. Let's look at a story that illustrates the effect of purpose.

Three men were busy laying bricks on a construction site. An observer approached. The first worker was dirty, sweaty, and had a miserable expression on his face. The observer asked him, "What are you doing?" He replied, "I'm laying bricks." The second worker was also dirty, sweaty, and miserable. The observer asked him, "What are you doing?" The second worker replied, "I'm earning twenty dollars an hour." The third worker was dirty and sweaty, too, but he had a joyful expression on his face. The observer asked him, "What are you doing?" He replied, "I'm building a cathedral."

It's so easy to lose touch with the deeper meaning of what you do every day. When you do, you put yourself at risk of frustration, burnout, and a feeling of emptiness that will undermine your enthusiasm and derail your sales efforts. When you remain conscious of your mission, you become energized. Instead of merely laying bricks or making money, you become motivated by what you are adding to your community and how you are contributing to people's lives.

After you become clear about your mission and the effect you want to have on others, you must write a mission statement. It doesn't have to be elegant, and it must be brief. It should explain in a few sentences the reason why your business exists. It should be simple enough for even an eight-year-old to understand.

Mission statements are as old as the Earth. The first mission statement, one that focuses completely on relationships, can be found in the Bible, in Genesis: "Be fruitful and multiply." That's a mission statement for mankind.

The Preamble to the Constitution of the United States established the purpose of the document: "We the People of the United States, in Order to form a more perfect Union, establish Justice, insure domestic Tranquility, provide for the common Defense, promote the general Welfare, and secure the Blessings of Liberty to ourselves and our Posterity, do ordain and establish this Constitution for the United States of America."

Another mission statement, probably equally familiar, is that of the Starship *Enterprise:* "To explore strange new worlds, to seek out new life and new civilizations, to boldly go where no man has gone before." In just a few seconds, millions of people watching *Star Trek* could understand what the show was about and why the Starship *Enterprise* existed. Can you communicate in just a few seconds why your business exists?

The mission statement is one of the most powerful sales and marketing tools you have. You can use it in your brochure, on your website, and in all your sales and marketing communications to position yourself and your business for success.

▶▶ ACTION STEP

WRITE YOUR MISSION STATEMENT

To write your mission statement, contemplate the following questions and write down your answers.

>> What do you do (other than selling)?

>> Who are your target clients?

>> What value or benefit do you bring to your clients?

>> What is your specialty or unique skill set?

>> Why do you do what you do? What is your contribution to society as a whole?

Refine your answers and create a two- or three-sentence mission statement. Evaluate your mission statement based on these criteria:

>> Does it describe your reason for being?
>> Is it short and easy to understand?
>> Would potential clients be attracted to your business after reading it?
>> Does it show how you provide more value or benefit than the competition? How you are unique?

The One-Minute Positioning Statement

Wouldn't it be great to have a powerful one-minute positioning statement you could use the next time you meet an ideal prospect? By instantly delivering a "conversational" mission statement, you could quickly establish yourself and your services accurately in the mind of the prospect.

Yet most financial professionals don't realize how much benefit they could gain from developing and using such a statement. For example, let's assume you're at a charity event filled with people in your particular target market—divorced and widowed women. One woman asks, "What do you do?" Most financial advisers fail to seize this opportunity to position themselves with their mission statement and attract a client effectively. Many answer, "I'm a financial consultant," "I'm an investment adviser," "I'm a life insurance salesman," or something equally uninteresting.

Instead, you want to say something that will get a response like this: "That sounds interesting. Tell me more." As you know, the first rule of selling is to attract attention and engage the prospect. The conversational mission statement fits the bill perfectly. You can use this powerful technique anytime, anywhere, to position yourself and your services in the mind of potential clients, in one minute or less.

This one-minute positioning, or OMP, consists of two parts, and each is essential to the positioning process. The first part begins with the words, "You know how ... " To complete this part, you describe your target market and the financial challenges its members might have. Consider these examples:

>> "You know how doctors spend many years in school and

training and then have limited time in which they can maximize their earnings?"

» "You know how small business owners have to invest much of their energy into building their business and have little time to spend properly handling their finances?"

» "You know how lots of divorced or widowed women are overwhelmed with the responsibility of dealing with their finances?"

Of course, you can adapt the specifics of your opening to position yourself with your target prospect. The power of this "You know how ... " opening builds on two important elements of sales psychology. First, rather than talking about yourself, you keep the focus on the prospect. In sales and marketing, it is much more important to be interested than interesting. Second, you reveal your understanding of the problems the prospect might face. Remember the adage, "Prospects don't care how much you care until they know how much you care."

The second part of the OMP begins with, "What I do is ... " This states the benefit of what you do and why your target prospect should do business with you. Don't confuse the benefit statement with a description of how you do your job. The "how" is important, but it doesn't belong in the OMP. Remember, the purpose of the OMP is to attract and engage prospects and compel them to want to learn more about what you do and how you do it. Here are a few examples of how to fill in the blanks:

» "What I do is help doctors make better financial decisions that will ensure their lifestyle long after their prime earning years are over."

» "What I do is help small business owners to preserve the financial success they have worked so hard for."

» "What I do is help divorced or widowed women take control of their finances and create a safe and secure financial future."

A good way to make sure the second part of your OMP is strong is to write it out, say it, and then ask, "So what?" For example, take the statement, "What I do is help doctors make better financial decisions." Give it the "So what?" test and you might come up with a more compelling statement, such as, "So they can have enough money to do everything they've ever dreamed of in their retirement years."

The second part of the OMP answers the most important question in any prospect's mind: "What's in it for me?" All prospects need the answer to this question before they will become your clients. How will you and your services make them feel happier, more secure, and more confident? How will you help them experience more financial freedom, or whatever their goals are?

Your OMP should follow the above guidelines and structure, even if the exact phrases seem limiting and contrived at first. After working within this structure for a while, you will develop thought patterns that will enable you to become more creative. The key here is to avoid discarding the structure too soon. The structure provides you with the classic problem/solution selling model. It also provides you with a benefit-positioning component for your target market. It is easy to lose the impact of these elements when you change the structure.

OMP is a powerful way to stand out among the competition, attract the attention of your ideal prospects, and let them know you can solve their problems. Take advantage of this effective technique the next time you meet someone you would like to have as a client. Your chances of closing will increase substantially when you start off with the right positioning for your business and mission statement.

 *POP QUIZ*

Choose the three statements that could be included in a mission statement.
   a. We make money.
   b. We make money selling people financial products and services.
   c. We make money selling lots of stuff.

d. We create financial security for our clients.

e. We make money selling lots of stuff to people.

f. We make money selling lots of financial stuff to people.

g. We provide our clients with peace of mind.

h. We make money selling lots of irrelevant financial stuff to people.

i. We make money selling lots of irrelevant financial stuff to uninformed people.

j. We help our clients achieve their investment dreams and goals.

EXECUTIVE SUMMARY

>> You may be an outstanding financial professional, but there are more than 500,000 other financial professionals out there going after the same clients.

>> Positioning or differentiating your business allows you to be seen and heard in an overcrowded marketplace.

>> A mission statement communicates the compelling reasons why a specific group of prospects should do business with you.

>> The best mission statements explain your purpose in a few words and are simple enough for a child to understand.

>> A one-minute positioning statement is a powerful way to attract and engage prospects and make them want to learn more about what you do and how you do it.

>> The mission statement and one-minute positioning statement continuously sharpen your own business strategy, objectives, product and service offerings, and targets.

---- ‖ ----

>> **Key to Success #3** is thinking your business through in totality by developing mission and one-minute positioning statements.

KEY 4

Go Long and Deep

Concentration is the key to economic results...
No other principle of effectiveness is violated as
constantly today as the basic principle of concentration...
Our motto seems to be: Let's do a little of everything.

—PETER DRUCKER

BUSINESSES THAT JUST GET BY ARE IN FOUR OR FIVE MARKETS. Businesses that do better are in three markets. Great businesses are in two markets, and phenomenal ones are in one market. It's a basic business premise to go long and deep in just one or two areas and get very good at it. Narrow your focus by target marketing.

Target marketing is based on your predetermined positioning in the marketplace. It is a methodology you enlist to reach your chosen clientele. Target marketing is the art and science of letting a specific group know you have what they want. Selling is the art and science of convincing these people to buy what you have. When you master these two skills and apply them concurrently, your potential is unlimited.

If you believe in the concept of positioning, as described in the previous chapter, but cannot decide on a target audience, here are a few guidelines for selecting one.

Pick a group with enough members. Your target market should be large enough for you to invest the time, energy, and resources to be successful. You must research the group you are considering and calculate how many clients you will need to meet your business goals. Corporate executives might be a good target market, but only if you can access enough of them effectively.

Select a market with resources. Your target market must have the money to buy your products and services. If you are selling fee-based investment products with high minimum investments, for example, you must limit yourself to the affluent market.

Don't fish in someone else's pond. Avoid target markets that are overprospected. If you chose doctors as a target, for instance, it is very likely they are being prospected on a regular basis. You will have more difficulty getting access to them, as well as increased competition. Ideally, you should find a potential market that has not yet been heavily mined.

There is no quick and easy way to find out if the market you are considering has been overprospected except by doing some research. If you find that most of the doctors to whom you are marketing have existing relationships, and they are satisfied with those relationships, try a specialty area, such as optometrists or dentists. You might find lots of opportunities simply by adjusting your sights slightly.

Look for good access. The target market should offer "leverageable" accessibility. This means the target group gathers together, has meetings, or has communication systems, such as newsletters and publications. For example, if you are targeting small business owners, leverageable accessibility could be a chamber of commerce, entrepreneurs' roundtable, or Rotary Club meeting that consists solely of small business owners.

Love the ones you're with. You should enjoy your target market. Most people spend more time with their clients and prospects than they do with their family and friends. If you don't enjoy spending time with your target market, there is a lot more at risk than your income level. If you are sharing your time with people you don't enjoy, you are risking the quality of your life.

For example, lawyers might be a lucrative target market, but you might not want to spend your days with them. Some lawyers can be ultraconservative, litigious, and obstinate. On the other hand, entrepreneurs can be an equally affluent market, and they might be more the type of people that you enjoy spending your time with. You might find them more enthusiastic and open to new ideas and risk taking. Given a choice of target markets that offer you equal earnings possibilities, wouldn't you rather be with people you like?

Get back to your roots. Start your target marketing journey based on where you're coming from. If you have a background in law or there are lawyers in your family, and you understand their personalities and professional challenges, lawyers might be a good target market. Similarly, if you love to play golf and are marketing to the affluent, this common interest could prove to be the right route for you. Likewise, a shared religious background might provide a perfect target market. Below are some ideas for possible target marketing opportunities.

» Small business owners (printers, restaurant owners, boat dealers, dry cleaners)
» Pre-retirees
» Self-employed professionals (dentists, veterinarians, consultants, architects)
» Entrepreneurs
» Salespeople (pharmaceutical reps, Mary Kay, real estate)
» Corporate executives (vice presidents and directors)
» People with a certain occupation (construction workers, teachers, firefighters)
» Ethnic groups (Koreans, Indians, Italians)
» Religious groups (Lutherans, Catholics, Jews)
» Affluent hobbyists (golfers, tennis players, trapshooters, boaters)
» Divorced women
» Widows
» Heirs
» Special interest groups (gardening groups, parent/teacher associations, car clubs)
» Members of charitable organizations

Once you've pinpointed your target market, you need some concrete strategies for reaching it. Here are the nine most effective strategic approaches to target marketing success.

1. *Interview current clients who are members of your target market.* Your current clients can provide you with a wealth of information, ideas, and contacts for expanding your penetration in your target market. (See the Action Step below for a more detailed strategy.)

2. *Identify and join your target market's professional associations and groups.* For example, if you are targeting restaurant owners, you could join a local chapter of a restaurant or hospitality professional association and attend meetings. Take a leadership role on a committee, and you'll be surrounded by precisely the prospects you are seeking as clients. Most professional associations welcome associates who provide products and services that are relevant to their members.

3. *Write for the target group's publications.* If your target market has a professional newsletter or magazine, provide articles or a monthly column with solutions to their financial concerns. Gain instant credibility.

4. *Speak at the group's meetings or conferences.* Most groups that have meetings are continually looking for individuals to provide programs for them. Some of these groups, such as the Rotary Club, hold regular lunch or dinner meetings and are eager to find speakers who can present relevant information to the members of their group. This, too, provides instant credibility.

5. *Get involved in the community.* Participate in common activities with your target group. Fundraisers, golf tournaments, and service work are powerful networking opportunities and can create a strong bond with members of your target market. You shine best when doing something for someone else.

6. *Conduct client events.* Client events provide the perfect opportunity to generate referrals in a nonpressured environment. Ask your clients to invite individuals from the same target market to attend your seminar, dinner, or special event, such as a golf outing.

7. *Promote public seminars.* Public seminars can be targeted to a specific group and can be a very effective target marketing strategy. For example, you could advertise a seminar for recently retired corporate employees on how to avoid tax problems with 401(k) plans. Some professional groups, such as accountants, insurance agents, and lawyers, are always in need of continuing-education credits. It is not difficult to become an accredited instructor and to promote lunch and dinner continuing-education seminars. These are perfect environments in which to meet your target market.

8. *Ask for referrals.* Most people know others just like themselves. Dentists know other dentists. Realtors know other realtor for referrals.

9. *Refer to your target market in all of your sales and marketing communications.* Identify your target market in your brochure, mission statement, and corporate overview, on your business card and website, and so forth.

One of the most important target marketing concepts is frequency of exposure. Most sales require asking for the business more than

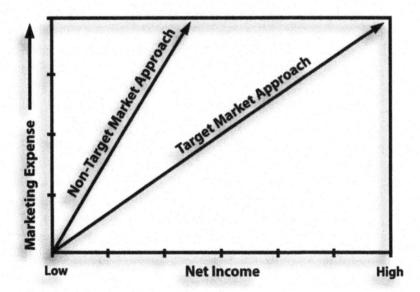

once. Most advertising budgets are based on multiple exposures, whether through radio, television, or print.

Likewise, applying more than one of the above strategies on a continuing basis will help ensure deep market penetration. Your marketing dollars will produce increased results because you are creating a powerful presence and awareness through repeated and frequent exposure to the same group. By contrast, the same amount of marketing dollars divided among many target markets will produce substantially less return.

▶▶ ACTION STEP

CREATE A CAB

Your Client Advisory Board is an informal group of your ideal clients who are willing to be interviewed and to provide you with advice, direction, and leads. Essentially, the CAB is a turbocharger for your target marketing efforts.

What's in it for your clients, you ask? Your clients will be motivated to become members of your CAB because you are recognizing them as worthy of providing advice. There are very few motivators that compare to making someone feel important. Many clients enjoy being advisers and meeting others like themselves, as well as having a complimentary lunch or dinner. As for you, you derive four powerful benefits from establishing a CAB.

Positioning. Your CAB will be composed of individuals who fit the market you have targeted. Through CAB meetings, you will position yourself and your business in those clients' minds far more effectively than you could with a brochure or website. After the advisory board conversation, your clients will be in a much better position to refer prospects and opportunities to you.

Also, by establishing a CAB, you will reaffirm your own commitment to your target market. After a few conversations with members of your advisory board that produce results, you will be motivated to increase your target marketing efforts. Success breeds success.

New clients. Because your CAB understands your ideal prospect, it will provide you with first-class referrals. In fact, CAB members will initiate the referrals and thus set the stage for face-to-face introductions or phone calls.

For example, if you ask a board member for referrals, and the response is, "You know, one of my suppliers would be a great contact for you. He has been concerned about the health care program he offers to his employees." At this point you say, "I would love to speak with him. Could you do me a big favor and just touch base with him and let him know I will be calling?" This is a referral that has enormous potential, because you are being introduced proactively rather than calling someone cold.

Valuable leads. Your CAB can provide you with contacts at professional associations, clubs, and organizations that are "nests" of your ideal prospects. You might not otherwise know what and where these groups are. Yet the groups that your ideal clients belong to are, in many cases, good groups for you to investigate. Simply ask your client, "What groups and organizations do you belong to?" Your client will direct you to the cluster of key professional organizations that you should know about.

New business opportunities with existing clients. Always keep in mind that your best opportunities for new business are your existing clients. And your CAB can be a great source of new business, because you will have a particularly close relationship with its members. For example, perhaps your business to date has centered on insurance but you have recently begun offering investment products. A CAB meeting is a perfect time to inform these key clients of your new offerings. Your clients might then want to set up individual meetings with you to discuss your new products and services.

Similarly, a CAB member might have developed a new financial-service need since you last spoke. If so, the next CAB meeting can trigger a mention of the new need and provide an opportunity for setting up a meeting to discuss it. For example, your client might recently have become a grandfather and want to discuss creating a college fund for his new grandchild.

—‖—

Now that you understand the advantages of a client advisory board, follow these steps to create one and begin reaping the benefits.

Step one: Identify your candidates. Make a list of candidates whom you would feel comfortable inviting to join your informal advisory board. They should fit your ideal client description. If you're not sure who your target market is, the client advisory list could be the catalyst for making that decision.

Ten to fifteen CAB members is ideal, but you might have to start with fewer. Remember: you are choosing clients whom you would like to clone.

Step two: Extend the invitations. Call each candidate and invite him or her to become a member of your advisory board. During this call you will explain the purpose of the board, what membership entails, and why you're asking this particular person to join. You will also present the call to action: an invitation to a lunch or dinner, during which you will begin the advisory relationship.

Here's an effective script that you can customize to fit your style and client relationship. "Mr. Choi, I need your help. You are the kind of client that I enjoy working with the most. I could really use your advice to help me attract more people like you, and also to learn how to serve you more effectively. I'm setting up an informal advisory board and hope that you will agree to join. Could we get together for lunch (or dinner) in the next few weeks?" In general, you want the invitation to sound informal yet important to them.

Once you have lined up your CAB members, decide how you want to conduct your meetings. You can meet with your board members individually or in small groups. Both formats work equally well. The advantage of the one-on-one meeting is the opportunity to spend quality time with each of your significant clients. However, when you meet as a group, the discussion tends to be livelier because of the group dynamic. Also, group meetings allow your clients to network with one another.

Logistics will also play an important role in how many people you invite. If you have clients scattered over large geographic areas, you might want to go to them individually, rather than adding the difficulty and inconvenience of travel to their participation. In other cases, clients may live or work near each other, and a group meeting can work very well.

If you can't decide, let your clients' preferences be the guiding consideration. Some people might prefer to meet with you alone, while others might enjoy networking with others. It's a good idea to review your list and give your clients a choice.

Step three: Conduct the first advisory meeting. First, thank your CAB member for taking the time to meet with you, and then reiterate that the purpose of the meeting is to help you attract more ideal clients, as well as to discover ways to serve this type of client more effectively.

Next, explain that you have a series of questions that will help you accomplish these goals. Below are a few key questions you should ask. Although you may think of others, these are highly focused, and you should consider using them when creating your own list.

» What professional relationships have been most valuable to you? Why?

» Are there any financial products I could offer, or is there anything else I could do to serve this community of clients more effectively?

» Do you belong to any professional organizations or clubs? If so, do you suggest I attend meetings or join any of them?

» What is the most important message to convey to individuals like you to attract their attention and interest in my services?

>> I'm interested in having more clients just like you. Where could I find more people like you?

>> If you were in my shoes, how would you market your services to attract clients like yourself?

>> Whom do you know who is like you and might be interested in learning about my services?

>> Can you recommend a good person who could give me information on attracting more clients like you?

Step four: Thank the advisory board member and develop an action plan. At the conclusion of the interview, it is important to again express your gratitude for the advice. You are sure to come up with a few items that require follow-up. You will probably need to get back in touch with your client fairly soon for contacts, referrals, and the like. Agree to a precise plan to follow up on the meeting.

If the meeting goes well, you can set yourself up for future meetings with the following script: "Mr. Choi, you've been extremely helpful. I really appreciate your agreeing to be a member of my informal client advisory board. Would it be all right for me to call you every so often to run some ideas past you and get some advice?"

As you can see, a CAB is a rich source of information on your target market and also presents great opportunities for new business with some of your best existing clients. It's also a great way to make these people feel special and valued. If you do a good job of pinpointing your target market, do your research, and use your CAB well, you are sure to achieve the target marketing success you're looking for.

POP QUIZ

1. Who makes more money?
   a. A general practitioner
   b. A cardiovascular surgeon
2. "Spray and pray" is an effective marketing strategy.
   □ True   □ False

3. A CAB is:

   a. A common mode of transport in large cities

   b. The part of a truck in which the driver sits

   c. An ideal way to increase client referrals

   d. All of the above

EXECUTIVE SUMMARY

» Most top producers have only one or two target markets.

» Your ideal target market should be large enough to be profitable, with members who can afford your products and are not already being well-served.

» You should enjoy the people in the market that you're targeting. Otherwise you're just setting yourself up for misery.

» Set up a client advisory board—an informal group of your ideal clients who are willing to provide you with advice, direction, and leads. Since your existing clients are your best resource, the advisory board will turbocharge your target marketing.

———‖———

» **Key to Success #4** is to deeply cultivate a client base by getting involved. You can't do it from your office chair or over the telephone. Get out into the community, create a CAB, and take every opportunity to speak to your target audience. This commitment is essential to maintaining a thriving business.

You've Got to Believe

*People may not remember exactly what you did
or what you said, but they will always remember
how you made them feel.*

—ANONYMOUS

THE DIFFERENCE BETWEEN A MODERATELY SUCCESSFUL AND a massively successful financial professional is not in what the individual knows. It is an inner quality, one that has the power to touch the prospect's emotional being.

Sales are made for emotional reasons and justified with logic. Selling is the transference of an emotion. That's why financial professionals must be absolute believers about the benefits of the product and services they are offering. You must "preach the gospel" with religious fervor. It's impossible to think you can inspire others to take action if you, in fact, are not inspired.

What inspires you—whether it's financial planning, asset allocation, modern portfolio theory, estate planning, whole life insurance, diversification, long-term care, market timing, or employee benefits—doesn't matter. What's important is you've got to believe in your heart that these products and services are right for your clients.

Logic and Emotion

The legendary jeweler Harry Winston is a great example of an evangelist in his field. One day he watched one of his salespeople lose a sale of a large diamond. As the customer headed for the door, Winston stopped him and engaged him further in a discussion of the stone he had been considering. Instead of rehashing the salesman's presentation, Winston described the stone as a symbol of exquisite beauty.

After speaking with Winston, the customer decided to buy the diamond. He was a bit confused by what had happened. He asked Winston why he'd been able to persuade him to make the purchase when the salesman hadn't. Winston replied, "The salesman is one of the best men in the business. He knows diamonds—but I love them." Winston was a believer and an evangelist who preached the gospel of diamonds.

You, too, must exude the evangelical spirit. The foundation of this spirit is the fundamental belief that the value of what you are selling far exceeds the cost. Without an honest belief in the superior value of your products or services, you have reduced your stature significantly, and the client will know it. When you believe, you are believed.

Financial evangelists are not in the business of selling objects. They are in the business of changing the quality of life of a group of important people. To the evangelist, every financial product and service becomes a cause to champion. Life, health, long-term care, and disability insurance are prerequisites for achieving clients' peace of mind and security. Investment products enable clients to live their retirement dreams and experience the joy of contributing to the lives of the people they love: children, grandchildren, and parents. Estate planning enables clients to leave the world a legacy and make the transition from success to significance. These are the reasons the financial professional becomes an evangelist. It's the good that you can do for others.

In almost every instance, you will know your products and services. That's a given. That's not enough. If knowledge could sell, the underwriters, money managers, and compliance officers would all be in the field selling. If facts and figures could sell, there would be no need for this book.

The truth is that facts and logic do not persuade the sale. Information in the form of opinions, facts, and figures can always be interpreted or misleading. It leads to the need for more information and the need for a second opinion. Selling from logic while excluding the emotions is selling from blindness. Client objections are the mind's automatic reaction to a selling presentation based solely on logic.

On the other hand, if you can connect your prospects with thoughts and ideas that trigger positive emotions, you will be selling from strength. They will feel positive about both you and what you are saying. They are connecting to you and trusting in you. Because they feel comfortable with you, they will have fewer objections, ones you can then handle with logic.

Get Connected to Your Clients

First, you must be emotionally connected to what you are selling. That will allow you to become creative in your approach, and this, in turn, will enable you to go a step further and address the emotional component of the sales process. You will be inspired, and you will reach out to touch the emotions of the prospect. In fact, your sales presentations will go more smoothly if you are a "believer" rather than a "seller." Why? Because you are selling from your heart: you want the best for your client.

For example, it makes sense for an individual to buy life insurance to protect the lives of his family members in the event of his unexpected death. Logically, you would think this is an issue most people would want to address. But no one wants to think about dying suddenly, and many people choose to avoid dealing with the possibility of this catastrophe. Many financial products and services are sold as contingencies in case something goes wrong in a client's life, so you are dealing with a client who is feeling pain about the future. Your job is to put the client at ease by starting with logic—everyone needs insurance—and then adding the emotional factor of how his or her family would fare without him.

But that's exactly the point: people don't always make decisions based on logic. In fact, more often they make decisions based at least partly on emotion and at least partly on their trust of you. Therefore, when you connect the prospect to the love, concern, and responsibility of caring for his spouse and family, the sale becomes emotionally driven instead of logically driven. The following story illustrates this point well.

A life insurance agent was trying to convince his friend of the importance of life insurance. He took the time to design the plan he felt would be the most beneficial for his friend's particular situation. The agent attempted every logical approach to closing the sale, based on his friend's needs.

Finally, in desperation, the agent came back to his friend and said, "OK, I've met my match. You do not see any good reason to purchase life insurance. But do me a favor. Will you sign this testimonial letter for me?"

His friend read the letter: "This is to confirm that I will not buy any life insurance from you, no matter how hard you try to convince me that I should."

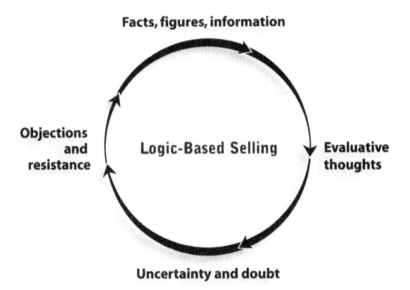

"What kind of a testimonial letter is this?" asked his friend. "To whom could you possibly want to show this?"

"I'll show it to your wife," said the agent. "Right after you die."

Needless to say, the agent closed the sale.

In the illustration at left, a sales presentation starts with information about the product or service. The first reaction of the prospect is serious thinking about what is being said, followed by a round of questions, leading to doubt and objections. This cycle continues until logic either wins or fails, and failure is more common. As we have noted, logic does not sell; emotions do.

In the second illustration below, logic is woven in with an emotional appeal for buying the product. This leads to positive thoughts about doing something good for one's family, followed by reduced fear and a decision to buy. As we will explain in the Action Step, there is one more factor the financial provider or adviser can use effectively and honestly to secure the sale. For now, remember Logic + Emotion.

Evangelists seize the opportunity to demonstrate their core belief system by taking action on what they preach. They are consumed by

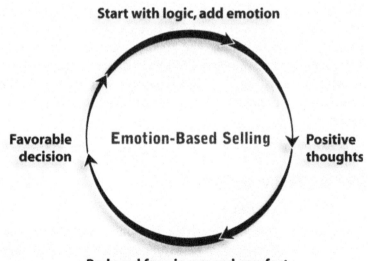

the cause they are selling. They are quick to let you know they own what they are asking you to buy. They walk the talk, practice what they preach, and are living examples of the personal, true value of their products and services.

The opportunity to buy what you sell and sell what you buy is a key advantage to working in the financial services industry. If you sold mainframe computers for IBM, you couldn't show a prospect the mainframe you bought for yourself and installed in your garage. If you worked for Boeing, you couldn't show a client the 747 you picked up over the weekend just because you believe so much in the aircraft business.

But in the financial industry, you can do that. You can show that you believe in, and act on, what you do. In fact, you can sell to others the idea that you too have bought using logic and emotion, regardless of whether it is a life insurance plan, an annuity, or a separately managed account. (In doing so, it is essential to state, of course, that your particular risk tolerance may differ from that of the prospect.)

When you sell something that you have bought, you take an intangible idea, process, concept, or belief system and make it tangible. Showing the prospect a financial plan or insurance or investment process that you've organized for yourself will sell far better than the most convincing factual presentation you could ever hope to deliver. This is how you testify to the truth of what you are doing. Start with the facts (logic), then weave emotion into your sales presentation, and finally conclude that you, too, have bought the same products and services. This is the most powerful sales cycle possible. It links product and service features and benefits, client emotion, and your personal touch in the sales presentation.

▶▶ ACTION STEP

WRITE YOUR BELIEFS

As a financial evangelist, the foundation for your existence is your belief system. It must be as immutable and unshakable as the Rock of Ages. Your ability to sell is based on a 100 percent belief in what you do and what you sell.

When you are totally clear about what you believe in, your presentations become inspired and your communication eloquent and filled with passion. So to help you define your "100 percent factor," write down all of your beliefs surrounding what you do and what you sell. Here are some examples:

» I believe retirement dreams can be achieved with proper planning.

» I believe every family deserves life insurance.

» I believe the government will not be able to care for the elderly.

» I believe the devastating effects of inflation and taxes can be avoided.

» I believe in a conservative approach to investing.

» I believe it is the responsibility of every person to provide quality care to aging parents.

Now fill one page with all of your beliefs, because your power to influence others resides in who you are. Reread this page every day for a month, and on any day you feel your faith might be fading.

❓ *POP QUIZ*

1. *Do you believe in your products?* ☐ Yes ☐ No
2. *Have you sold them to your family?* ☐ Yes ☐ No
3. *Do you feel your business is a calling?* ☐ Yes ☐ No
4. *Do you believe you are changing lives?* ☐ Yes ☐ No

If you answered "yes" to all these questions, you are a financial evangelist. Hallelujah!

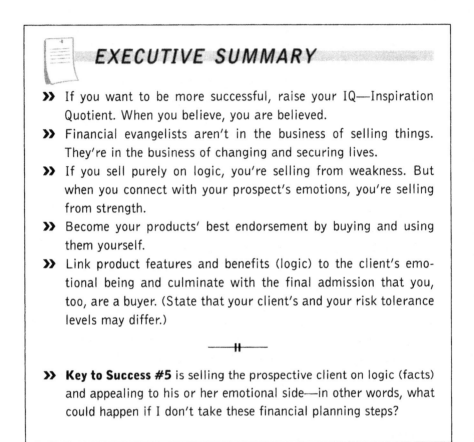

EXECUTIVE SUMMARY

» If you want to be more successful, raise your IQ—Inspiration Quotient. When you believe, you are believed.

» Financial evangelists aren't in the business of selling things. They're in the business of changing and securing lives.

» If you sell purely on logic, you're selling from weakness. But when you connect with your prospect's emotions, you're selling from strength.

» Become your products' best endorsement by buying and using them yourself.

» Link product features and benefits (logic) to the client's emotional being and culminate with the final admission that you, too, are a buyer. (State that your client's and your risk tolerance levels may differ.)

———H———

» **Key to Success #5** is selling the prospective client on logic (facts) and appealing to his or her emotional side—in other words, what could happen if I don't take these financial planning steps?

Don't Be Afraid
to Walk Away:
Jim's Epiphany

You've got to know when to hold 'em, know when to fold 'em,
Know when to walk away and know when to run.

—KENNY ROGERS

WHEN I FIRST STARTED OUT IN SELLING, WHICH WAS A COUPLE of years after I started in the home office, I had absolutely nothing going for me. I was told that success in the business was like running a marathon. You've got to be tough, diligent, and persistent, and above all never give up. You've got to learn how to hang in there.

In fact, I can summarize my experiences in those first few years as a form of sophisticated begging. Every day I was out there groveling. It took me about three years before I had an epiphany about selling. It was based on a specific experience with a particular prospect.

It all began when an accountant referred me to a fellow named Rich. He was about thirty-eight years old. He and his wife, Julia, had two kids and lived nearby. Rich worked for a major real estate company in the area. He had a significant income, and he was described to me as a first-class referral.

I called him and asked if I could come by his office to talk to him about the work that I did. He agreed and suggested we get together over lunch. That sounded great to me.

We met at a restaurant that was actually a little too expensive for my limited budget in those days. We had great rapport. I liked Rich, and he seemed to like me, too. I walked him through the financial-planning process. He seemed impressed and agreed to a fact-finding interview right on the spot.

We went through an hour-long fact finder. He revealed an enormous amount of information. At the end of the lunch, I said, "Could we get back together next week? I'll put together some tentative findings." This was my selling process at the time. I'd come back with two plans and move to a trial close, asking for my prospect to take action on one of the plans I presented. Rich agreed to meet again.

I asked if we could meet at his office, and Rich said, "Can we have lunch?" I liked how things were moving along in the sales process and said, "Lunch, sure. Let's have lunch." I was excited and could taste the looming sale.

So we set a time and date, and we had lunch again. We met at the same restaurant. I picked the same table, for good luck. We talked about both of the plans I had carefully put together for him. Rich liked Plan A and agreed to move forward in finalizing it.

I explained what I would be doing; we talked about the details that I would need to confirm and how the program would be structured when it was complete. Rich seemed to be totally on board with the program and suggested we meet and have lunch again.

So we met again for lunch at the same restaurant and same table. I was feeling as if I had gained a few unwanted pounds from all these expensive lunches but was also optimistic about being nearer to closing this piece of new business.

We sat down and reviewed the parts of the plan we had agreed to discuss. It was mostly a matter of confirming a variety of details and finalizing them. Toward the end of our lunch Rich confessed, "You know, Jim, I'm having a lot of problems with my wife. Julia just does not want to go ahead with this plan. She's very down on it. Believe it or not, we're having a cash-flow problem right now. But the biggest problem is that part of this plan involves buying insurance, and she doesn't feel we are in a position to throw any money into insurance."

This was a new wrinkle I hadn't foreseen, but it didn't seem like an insurmountable obstacle. "Listen," I said, "I apologize to you and your wife. Julia should have been part of this process, and she probably feels excluded. Your wife is a very valuable partner, not only in your life, but also in the planning process. Maybe if you, she, and I got together, we could restructure this so it makes sense to everyone."

"Ah, well," Rich hesitantly replied, "let me talk to her myself, and I'll report back to you. Let's get back together for lunch in about a week." So about a week later we got back together for our fourth lunch. We met again at Rich's favorite restaurant. I couldn't help but think about the cost, because these lunches were beginning to add up. I was spending more than I had been accustomed to.

As soon as we sat down, Rich reported sadly, "No, my wife won't go ahead. She is very down on this. I think we have to just forget the whole thing."

"Rich, I don't want to forget the whole thing," I persisted. "Let's just skip this whole lunch thing. It doesn't seem to be working for either of us. Why don't we take a ride to your house right now? I'd like an opportunity to talk with your wife for a few moments."

My coaxing was successful. Rich agreed to bring us all together that day, and we went to his house. I brought along my presentation folder, which outlined the plan and all the benefits of my proposal. I sat down with Julia, and we started talking.

As I began speaking, I instantly realized she didn't have a clue who I was or what I was talking about. She didn't know anything about the plan whatsoever. In fact, she thought I was the guy who had sold them their automobile insurance.

Following the guidelines of selling that I had been taught, I persevered. I patiently went through my presentation, explaining how the planning process worked, how the various products worked to their benefit, and how the value of what I was suggesting far outweighed any costs associated with the plan.

I guess I had done a good job putting the plan together and presenting it, because at the end she looked up and said, "Rich, this makes a lot of sense. Based on our cash flow and how we have been handling our finances until now, this plan could provide us with a lot more control and security. I really like it. Let's talk about putting this plan into action."

You can imagine how elated I was. "Terrific!" I chimed in. "Rich, now that both you and Julia are on board, let's talk about the steps we need to take to finalize this plan."

Rich immediately jumped in, "No, no, I've got another problem. It's my accountant." At this point I was stupefied and totally beyond my patience zone. "Wait a minute," I retorted. "Your accountant is *my* accountant, and he is the one who referred me to you in the first place! And I know he approves of and recommends the kind of plan I'm presenting to you today."

"He likes it for you; he doesn't like it for me," Rich responded.

I managed to maintain my "never take no for an answer" attitude for a few more minutes of arguing. Ordinarily, I would have hung in there for an hour or two, going back over all of the objections. But something happened. I was blinded by a brilliant thunderbolt of truth.

I just sat there for a moment as I processed what I was experiencing. Instead of plodding onward like a private in Custer's army, I closed my presentation book and stood up to leave. As I did, Rich got very annoyed.

You see, Rich was having fun humiliating a salesperson. He didn't have any respect for someone selling financial products. At that moment he was having fun humiliating me in front of his wife and wanted it to continue. He demanded to know where I was going.

I was in a rush to get out the door, but before I walked out, I said, "Rich, I'm not sure you know what's been happening over the last four or five lunches we've had together. Presumably you've been deciding whether or not you want to do business with me. But maybe you haven't understood what I've been doing.

"Rich, I've dedicated my entire life to serving the needs of my well-selected clients. I work with them on financial planning, insurance, and estate planning. I take this business very, very seriously. I'm dedicated to improving the lives of my clients and, believe it or not, my clients are dedicated to me. And so over the last few weeks, I've been going through a decision-making process, too. I've been deciding whether or not you qualify to be part of my clientele. And I've decided you don't make the cut."

The day I walked out of Rich's house was the most self-empowering event of my entire twenty-five years in the business. It took me seven years to learn this lesson. If you are new to the business, you can save a lot of time by learning this lesson faster than I did. Time is irreplaceable, and it is your most valuable resource. Don't throw it away on insincere, disrespectful prospects.

What we do has dignity. We are professionals, and this is a noble and admirable profession. It has value. It has tremendous meaning to those who engage our services. You should be sharing your time, skills, and expertise only with people who truly care about their financial opportunities and your effort and time.

▶▶ ACTION STEP

BECOME A MASTERFUL QUALIFIER

High achievement in selling hinges on investing your time properly. Qualifying—the process of identifying someone who has both the need and the ability to buy from you—will enable you to invest your most valuable possession in the most profitable way.

Qualifying is the single most important skill in selling. If you implement it skillfully, you can double, triple, and quadruple your income. On the other hand, qualifying poorly could mean your speedy exit from the business.

Regardless of your experience, it's easy to waste time with prospects who are not qualified and are unlikely to ever become your clients, for one reason or another. Failure to close is often the by-product of failure to qualify. It's easy to mistake pretenders for contenders. Here are five guidelines for qualifying prospects more effectively.

1. Identify prospects who have used your products or services before. People who have a history of purchasing your product or service in the past are more likely to purchase it in the future.

2. Find out what your clients like about the products or services they have. This will reveal how much they value your product or service and how much they are predisposed to purchasing what you are offering. For example, individuals who have purchased life insurance products in the past and are satisfied with their decision are much more likely to buy again in the future.

3. Find out what they didn't like about products or services they have purchased from other people in the past. For example, maybe they engaged the services of a financial adviser but were disappointed by the lack of contact and communication with this adviser. This information will give you important ammunition that you should use when closing the sale. In this scenario, if you have lots of communication built into your business model, you will want to highlight how you are offering the one feature that is especially important to the prospect. You'll also quickly find out if this individual will be a problem client.

Using the same example, you might find out, on further questioning, that the prospect had unreasonable expectations of a financial adviser. This information should definitely be a red flag. Such an individual has the potential to become a problem client and for this reason doesn't qualify.

4. Identify who is involved in making the final decision. Usually family financial decisions are made jointly by the husband and wife. In other cases, accountants or other advisers need to be involved. Don't waste time presenting without including all the principals in the process.

5. Find out if they are ready, or when they would be ready, to take action. Use a customized version of this script: "If we were fortunate enough to come up with the right plan that would enable you to (retire comfortably, send your kids to college), would you be in a position to proceed by (next week, next month)?"

The Real Truth about Some Prospects

» Some prospects are quick to agree to free lunches at expensive restaurants.

» Some prospects do not always reveal their true feelings.

» Some prospects believe their time is more valuable than yours is.

» Some prospects assume canceling an appointment is unimportant.

» Some prospects are not honest all the time.

» Some prospects are misleading, whether inadvertently or intentionally.

» Some prospects occasionally tell a nontruth.

» Some prospects are slow to trust you with all of their financial information immediately.

 *POP QUIZ*

1. *Jim should have known after the second lunch that Rich was leading him on.*   ☐ True   ☐ False

2. *Jim should have engaged Rich's wife earlier in the process and pushed for a close.*   ☐ True   ☐ False

3. *Jim should have thought more carefully about Rich's response to the selling process.*   ☐ True   ☐ False

4. *Through all the expensive lunches and his investment of time Jim learned a valuable lesson: Know when to walk away.*   ☐ True   ☐ False

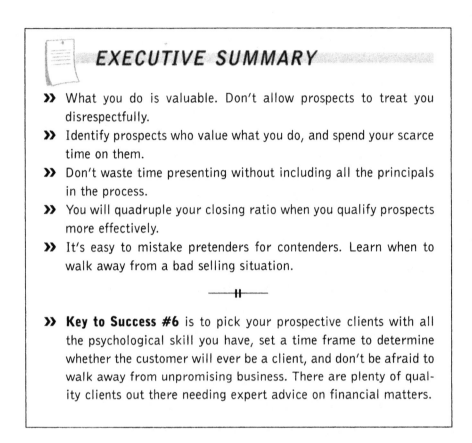

EXECUTIVE SUMMARY

» What you do is valuable. Don't allow prospects to treat you disrespectfully.

» Identify prospects who value what you do, and spend your scarce time on them.

» Don't waste time presenting without including all the principals in the process.

» You will quadruple your closing ratio when you qualify prospects more effectively.

» It's easy to mistake pretenders for contenders. Learn when to walk away from a bad selling situation.

———**╫**———

» Key to Success #6 is to pick your prospective clients with all the psychological skill you have, set a time frame to determine whether the customer will ever be a client, and don't be afraid to walk away from unpromising business. There are plenty of quality clients out there needing expert advice on financial matters.

Give Them Something to Say "Yes" To

To be simple is the best thing in the world; to be modest is the next best thing. I am not so sure about being quiet.

—G. K. CHESTERTON

LOTS OF SALES TAPES AND TRAINING PROGRAMS SUGGEST closing phrases and magical closing scripts. Many of these phrases can be useful to include in your sales process. But one of the most powerful strategies you can apply during the closing process is to give your buyer something that's easy to say yes to.

Many financial products and plans are complicated and difficult to understand. Even financial professionals can be challenged when faced with the broad range of financial products, to first completely understand and then communicate the information in a way the prospect or client can comprehend. Remember, consumers aren't exposed to financial concepts and products every day, so your presentation is going to be new to them and more likely than not hard to grasp the first time through, especially if they're not technically inclined.

Consequently, it's not unusual for the financial professional to get lost in a maze of product features and technical details that create confusion in the mind of the prospect. Multiple dry runs before the actual presentation can help, but the fact remains that complicated or technical presentations, by their very nature, are problematic and can create significant obstacles to closing the sale.

Even if your presentation is perfect and the client understands exactly what you have said, he is unlikely to make a final decision in front of you. First he will discuss your recommendations with his accountant, lawyer, spouse, business partner, friends, associates, or other advisers. Because you are not even present at those discussions, it is impossible for you to help close this part of the sale.

What you *can* do to help yourself is to create agreement on at least part of what you are recommending. Then when prospective clients take your suggestions away with them to think about, they already have something to say yes to.

Perhaps your idea, concept, or recommendation can be distilled down to a simple question that is easy to understand and to communicate. What is the benefit of your plan or product? What pain will be relieved as a result of accepting your proposal?

Here are ten examples of questions you can weave into your presentation that are easy to say yes to:

1. Do you want me to reduce your taxes?
2. Do you want to maintain your current lifestyle after you retire?
3. Do you want to provide quality care to your parents in their later years?
4. Do you want to contribute to your children's education?
5. Do you want to leave a meaningful legacy to a cause or institution?
6. Do you want the security of guaranteed income in your later years?
7. Do you want to avoid the crisis of outliving your money?
8. Do you want to control whether your estate gets transferred to your loved ones or to the government?
9. Do you want to neutralize the effect of inflation on your assets and avoid unnecessary taxes?
10. Do you want a free second opinion on your financial plan?

These are just a few examples of questions that will evoke the yes you are seeking during your sales presentation and even afterward, when your prospective client takes your suggestions away to think about. Everyone needs an EYQ—an easy-yes question. Your objective is to create agreement that will move the sale closer to conclusion. If you are new to the business, develop a few irresistible EYQs. If you are more experienced, you may not be conscious of your EYQ, and it might need refinement or more consistent application.

The Six-Point Proposal System

At some point in your selling process you will need to present your recommendations in a detailed summary, as a follow-up or adjunct to the verbal presentation. To close more sales, you need a technique that will enable you to take complex ideas, plans, proposals, or recommendations and communicate them in a form that will help you get the "big yes" you are looking for. Our powerful six-point proposal system spells out the process for you.

Regardless of whether you are presenting to one person or a group, this system will enable you to communicate the most effectively. Its simplicity (and therefore its persuasiveness) is reflected in its brevity. All six points must fit on one sheet of paper.

1. **The recommendation.** Write down, in one sentence, the proposal and action you are suggesting the client should take. What is the basic idea you are seeking to communicate?

2. **The reasons.** Why are you asking the prospective client to take the recommended action? Write down the two or three reasons, based on the client's financial situation, that you are recommending this product or service.

3. **The results.** What two or three major benefits to the client would result from accepting your recommendation?

4. **The cost.** What cost is associated with your recommendation? It is important to be clear and reveal all charges that your recommendation will incur. Include all commissions and fees. Consider adding a sentence that describes the "opportunity cost"—benefits that would be lost if the client didn't follow your recommendation.

5. **The alternatives.** What two or three other options did you thoughtfully consider before making the recommendation you are putting forth? Write down the other possibilities you might have

chosen to present to the prospective client and why you didn't. It is important to demonstrate that you have considered a variety of other options. Step five builds credibility in your proposal by showing the prospective client that you did your homework.

6. **The implementation timetable.** What are the exact steps that need to be taken to put the recommendation into place? It is vital to make sure the prospective client understands that he or she has obligations if the proposal is accepted.

The next time you present a proposal, organize it using the six-point system. You'll be amazed at how well you are able to communicate your recommendation. You'll present your suggestions in a form that will make them easy to say yes to.

▶▶ ACTION STEP

BEGIN USING THE SIX-POINT PROPOSAL SYSTEM

Here is an example of what a six-point proposal for an investment portfolio might look like.

1. Alex, you have stated that you want a diversified investment portfolio. I recommend that you now put 20 percent of your liquid assets into the health care sector.

2. The reason for this recommendation is that the health care sector is expected to grow at 9 percent per year over the next five years, whereas the S&P index is expected to grow at 6 percent over the same time period. In addition, the aging population will create a new, large market for pharmaceuticals, medical devices, and medical services, including HMOs and hospitals.

3. The result of implementing this proposal will be that, while past market performance is no guarantee of future performance, your portfolio could gain the potential to outpace the general equity market by three percentage points. You will also diversify out of the more narrow selections we have decided on in the past.

4. I recommend that you purchase $75,000 of the Lincoln health care equity fund; 1,000 shares of Dyna pharmaceuticals; and 1,500 shares of Thomson health care systems. Lincoln has had a five-year growth rate of 12 percent, and the two stocks I recommend have price points 15 percent higher than today's market price.

5. I looked at other equity funds but was not happy with the turnover of the fund managers nor with their growth rates. I considered Lafayette Aggressive fund and Williams Healthcare Growth fund. Both were inferior to Lincoln in terms of rate of return. Among stocks there are many choices, but the two I recommend have deep product pipelines, and Thomson also has prospects for further acquisitions. Lincoln, Dyna, and Thomson are likely to be solid performers in the next five years. I know you describe yourself as moderately conservative. These investments fit that model, as does the 20 percent figure.

6. I recommend that you sell $125,000 of your position in Global Technology Fund, which has gained over the period you have owned it but now, I believe, as do my analyst colleagues, will start to underperform. I would suggest we meet on Monday to discuss this proposal in my office, and if you approve, make the sale on Tuesday. As in the past, we will meet monthly to review your portfolio's performance. I know how important it is for you to have total information about your financial status.

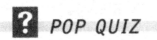 *POP QUIZ*

Which of the following questions are likely to get a yes?

a. Are you a glutton for high commissions?

b. Would you like to invest $100,000 in a start-up Internet company?

c. Does network marketing turn you on?

d. You don't want to do business with me, do you?

Can't find any EYQs among the above? Go back and reread the chapter, and learn to ask questions that your prospect can say yes to!

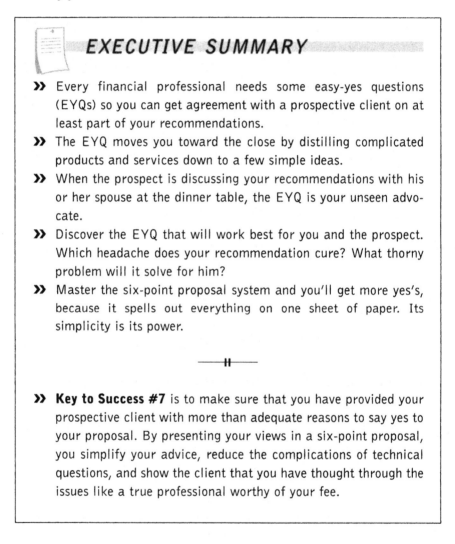

EXECUTIVE SUMMARY

» Every financial professional needs some easy-yes questions (EYQs) so you can get agreement with a prospective client on at least part of your recommendations.

» The EYQ moves you toward the close by distilling complicated products and services down to a few simple ideas.

» When the prospect is discussing your recommendations with his or her spouse at the dinner table, the EYQ is your unseen advocate.

» Discover the EYQ that will work best for you and the prospect. Which headache does your recommendation cure? What thorny problem will it solve for him?

» Master the six-point proposal system and you'll get more yes's, because it spells out everything on one sheet of paper. Its simplicity is its power.

——**††**——

» Key to Success #7 is to make sure that you have provided your prospective client with more than adequate reasons to say yes to your proposal. By presenting your views in a six-point proposal, you simplify your advice, reduce the complications of technical questions, and show the client that you have thought through the issues like a true professional worthy of your fee.

Develop a
Marketing Rhythm

*What if one does say the same things, of course in a
little different form each time, over and over? If he has anything
to say worth saying, that is just what he ought to do.*

—OLIVER WENDELL HOLMES

TWO TYPES OF PEOPLE ARE SUCCESSFUL AT SELLING. INTER-
estingly enough, they are on opposite ends of the intelligence
continuum. On one end are very methodical, dull people. And yet
some of these people are quite successful. The reason they are successful is they know they are a bit slow, so when they find something
that works, they just keep doing it. Month after month, year after
year, they just keep working their system. They find that they develop a rhythm and a cadence, and it's fun. They are afraid to branch
out too much, because there is comfort in continuity, and they know
there is a good chance they could fail at anything new. There are no
experimenters in this group; they simply follow the same strategy
with every client. The drawback to this method, of course, is that all
clients are not alike, so salespeople in this group often fail with new
customers because their selling isn't client-centered.

A second kind of person is also very successful at selling financial products. The people in this category, by contrast, are extremely
intelligent. In fact, they are so smart and have so much wisdom and

perspective that they realize the only way to be really successful is to do things exactly like the slow, methodical people—*find something that works and then keep on doing it.*

Unfortunately, most of us fall somewhere in between. We are not dumb enough to get it and not smart enough to get it. We are always moving in lots of different directions, trying new things, going into new markets, and exploring new strategies and techniques. Without a strong background rhythm, we don't create consistency and sustainability. It's important to find a sales approach you can apply time and time again.

Tony Bennett has sung "I Left My Heart in San Francisco" more than 15,000 times professionally. He always leaves his heart in San Francisco. He never leaves it in Cincinnati or Salt Lake City. He never leaves it anywhere else. In an interview he once said, "I love singing that song. I can sing it forever." And that is what creates sales success. Find something you love to do, and do it over and over and over again.

You must discover the process that you love, the song that you can sing forever. If you love it, it will feel like a groove and not a rut. Why would you want to stop? Why change? If you found something in your personal life that worked, like a great golf swing, you wouldn't want to change it. You would want to keep repeating it.

Look at Ray Kroc, one of the greatest success stories in American business. Kroc created McDonald's, the most lucrative restaurant chain in U.S. business history. What makes his story even more compelling is that he broke the most revered rule in business: Create a better mousetrap, and the world will beat a path to your door.

Kroc didn't create a better product, he created a questionable one. Let's face it: very few people would be willing to say a McDonald's hamburger is a fantastic hamburger. In fact, it would have to be rated mediocre by even the most lenient standards. Based on his hamburgers alone, Kroc could never have achieved the success he did. But that's not what he was selling.

He understood that the product was only one component in the success of a small business. Ray Kroc realized that most small businesses fail not because of the quality of the product but because of the systems that manage the business of the business. Kroc invented good systems—fast systems to give people on the go what they wanted. Kroc produced a prototype that was idiot-proof: the turnkey business. Each owner of a McDonald's franchise simply has to follow the instructions.

Kroc created systems that could duplicate results again and again.

The key to ongoing and unlimited success in the financial industry is to create sales and marketing systems the way Ray Kroc did. You need sales systems to attract and close high-quality business, follow-up systems to make sure your clients are cared for, learning systems to make sure you are at the head of the class. All of these systems must be reproducible ad infinitum. In fact, you shouldn't even have to think about putting these systems into effect; they should occur automatically in your practice.

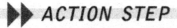

▶▶ ACTION STEP

IDENTIFY YOUR SYSTEM

How do you know if your systems are working? Very simply, over time you get better at what you do: serving people's financial needs. If your practice doesn't run smoothly, if you don't have a cohesive system, or if your current system needs work, follow this simple six-part exercise to help you identify the ideal business system for you and your business model—one that duplicates itself over and over again.

1. Make two lists of five to ten of your best clients. Put the clients that are the most lucrative on one list, and the ones that are the most professionally enjoyable to work with on the other.

2. Next, track the evolution of these clients. How did you secure each one? Include in your analysis the circumstances under which you were introduced, other individuals who played a role, what you said, and any specific strategies or techniques you applied. If the client came through a passive referral, identify the strategies and techniques you applied to acquire the original client.

3. Rate the efficiency and desirability of your marketing systems. Perhaps you secured some clients through inefficient marketing strategies. For example, you may have acquired an excellent client through a booth you took at a trade show. Your return on investment—one client—may not warrant repeating this strategy.

Likewise, canvassing a target neighborhood door-to-door may have landed you a great client who is a small business owner. But such canvassing may not be the most efficient investment of your time. Obtaining one client, albeit a good one, does not merit focusing a lot of time and energy on this strategy.

Similarly, you may have used cold calling as a prospecting strategy. Cold calling works, but you might not enjoy it. It takes a certain personality to make cold calling an effective part of your marketing system.

On the other hand, if you acquired two or three of your best clients from seminars you presented, and the return on your investment of both time and money was substantial, you should seriously consider making seminars a big component of your marketing system.

4. Earmark the strategies that resulted in success and efficiency, make them part of your marketing system, and forget about everything else. Keep in mind that there aren't twenty-five effective marketing strategies. There probably aren't even fifteen, when it comes right down to it. Below are the most common marketing strategies for financial products and services. Some are more appropriate to use in the beginning of your career, while others are more applicable after you have been in business for a while. Some work best for specific products or services.

» Cold calling
» Direct mail
» Seminars
» Client events
» Referrals
» Strategic alliances with CPAs and attorneys
» Door-to-door canvassing

>> Buying leads
>> Public relations
>> Advertising
>> Trade shows

Consider the "e-factor"—the enjoyment factor—as well as the effectiveness of each marketing strategy. Human nature means we are most likely to repeat what we really enjoy. For example, everyone knows how hard it is to maintain an exercise program over the long term, but if you choose an activity you enjoy, you're more likely to stick with it. It's the same with sales techniques.

Choose one or perhaps two marketing strategies that you enjoy the most. You might have to explore a few in-depth to find out which ones work for you. Remember that trial and error is your best approach to finding what works well for you.

5. Create a prototype. Even the most effective sales and marketing system needs to be refined. Think of your sales and marketing system as a franchise. If you purchased a Rug Cleaning "R" Us franchise, they would give you not only the equipment you needed but also a step-by-step process for marketing the business. They would tell you where and how to advertise, how to create repeat clients, how to generate referrals, and so forth.

Now transfer this concept to your financial business. If you have identified a system that brings in the kinds of clients you want, break the system down into the exact steps that you need to take to duplicate the results. To do this effectively, you will probably need to test various elements until you have optimized your results.

For example, with a seminar-selling strategy, you might want to test such variables as using mailing lists versus direct invitations, presenting on different days of the week, giving mini-seminars at the local Rotary club, and so on until you find the optimal mix for your business. Sales and marketing is both an art and a science, so avoid the trap of paralysis by analysis and start testing your prototype.

In building your prototype, it is extremely important to document each part of your process. Using the example of seminars, you can document a timeline for seminar implementation, outlining when to prepare the invitations, when to mail, when to reserve the room, and—what's most important—when and how to follow up. Then document the procedure for taking reservations, confirming reservations, setting appointments, and so on. You should also document your seminar script.

The benefits of creating a prototype are twofold. First, you will have a record of what you are doing and can measure results. When you want to adjust or tweak your system, you can compare various approaches and make improvements. Second, if you document your marketing system, you will able to delegate portions of it.

6. Create a plan for implementing your strategy repeatedly. Along the way, you can and should continue to refine your prototype and improve the efficiency of your system.

It is advisable to seek wise counsel for feedback during this step. Talk to colleagues who have applied this strategy successfully. Seek out training and coaching programs that focus on the skills needed for implementing your system. Remain open and teachable. Knowing what you don't know can help you to improve your results exponentially. Refine, amend, and adjust your marketing system, and you'll soon find that you are getting the results you've been seeking.

 **POP QUIZ**

From the list below, choose the four most cost-effective and reproducible systems for marketing a financial products and services business.

a. Run television ads during the Super Bowl.

b. Conduct seminars offering financial solutions for your target market.

c. Hope the phone rings after you've placed a small ad in your local newspaper.

d. Drive around in a truck like the ice cream man, playing "Money" by the Beatles.

e. Generate referrals by cloning your ideal clients.

f. Look at your computer screen for hours on end.

g. Become active with targeted charitable and nonprofit groups.

h. Create strategic alliances with CPAs and attorneys.

i. Pray and wait.

EXECUTIVE SUMMARY

» Find a system that works.

» Find a marketing system you love.

» Do it over and over and over again.

» Embrace predictability. Know what works ahead of time. But don't be afraid to tweak your system to make it even better. Remember that you are working in a dynamic, competitive marketplace with prospective clients entering and leaving all the time.

———**H**———

» **Key to Success #8** is to find a marketing system that suits your personality, your marketplace, and your way of doing business, such as aggressive versus laid-back. Once you have found a group of tactics or sales elements that work, stick to them, but every so often try to think of how to do things better. Remember Ray Kroc.

Follow the
60-20-20 Rule

Creativity is thinking up new things.
Innovation is doing new things.

—THEODORE LEVITT

AFTER YOU HAVE GOTTEN YOUR FINANCIAL SERVICES BUSINESS up and running, it is not unusual to discover that your income has reached a plateau. You may attempt to break free and improve your production by working harder, only to find it doesn't produce the results you are looking for.

In some cases, to add to your frustration, your productivity can actually *decrease* because of changes in the marketplace or changes in the demand for your product or service. You are caught up in what we call repeated-activity-result syndrome, as illustrated in the diagram on the following page. In this scenario, it is easy to get frustrated or even suffer from burnout, because you are on a treadmill that goes nowhere.

The most powerful strategy for breaking this inertia and jump-starting your sales again is to follow the 60-20-20 Rule. This rule allows you to continue performing the activities that are creating sales while also discovering, testing, and initiating new techniques to increase sales even more. It entails the following approach to time management:

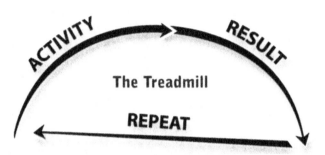

Spend 60 percent of your time implementing your current sales and marketing systems. These are the activities that you can almost do in your sleep. They include your prospecting strategies, scripts, closing techniques, and so on.

Spend 20 percent of your time on pure research, learning about things that may or may not have a practical application. Study new technical information, target markets, products, applications, scripts, marketing strategies, referral methodologies, selling techniques, new business models, and so forth.

Your research could entail any number of activities. But regardless of the type of research you do, you must maintain an attitude of openness and curiosity to conduct it effectively. Ignore your inner voice of judgment while you explore new ideas so you can avoid discarding an idea before giving yourself a chance to fully investigate its potential. With that in mind, include the following four important sources of information in your research.

1. Books. Look for books that are narrowly focused on the topic you are researching. For example, if you are exploring Internet marketing, try to find books on how financial professionals can use the Internet to market their services.

2. The Internet. Using search engines, you can gather an enormous amount of valuable information on the topic of your choice in a matter of minutes. You can access appropriate websites, retrieve articles, and connect with experts and other information sources.

3. Trade and professional associations. Contact the appropriate group and ask for information on the topic you are exploring. For instance, groups such as the Financial Planning Association, the National Association of Financial and Estate Planning, the American Association of Long-Term Care Insurance, and the Association of Health Insurance Advisors can be great sources for specific product and application information. Even if they cannot provide you with exactly what you're looking for, they can often point you in the right direction.

4. Interviews. Interview people who have had experience with the subject at hand. Network locally and contact people whom you want to know more about. For example, if you are considering establishing strategic alliances with CPAs or estate planning attorneys, you could interview them to understand their needs and concerns and to discuss how you could work together. In this case, you would also want to interview colleagues who have created successful strategic alliances with CPAs and attorneys, to find out how they established the relationships and how profitable the relationships have been.

Spend the remaining 20 percent of your time applying the research that makes sense. The ideas that work should be rolled into the activities on which you focus 60 percent of your time, efforts that you already know will work. At the same time, you should continue to evaluate your 60 percent segment and drop the activities, products, and services that are not working as well as they once did.

By continuing to do what has generally worked well, researching new ideas, implementing the ones with potential, and refining your process, you will get off the treadmill and enter the cycle of growth, as in the illustration on the following page.

You don't have to follow the exact percentages, but divide your time among these three activities to help you innovate and find new ways to grow your business. Spend most of your time doing what works. Spend some time researching new possibilities, and spend some time testing and innovating your business. You'll keep your entrepreneurial spirit alive.

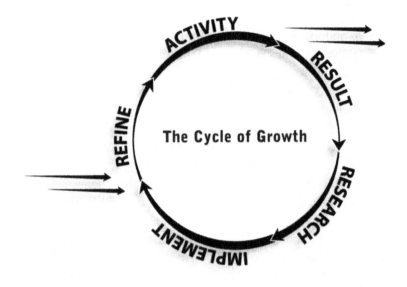

▶▶ ACTION STEP

RESEARCH GROWTH ACTIVITIES

Below are some sales- and marketing-related strategies for growing your business. Keep doing what works, but choose one from the list to research, test, implement, and refine.

- ❯❯ Begin a direct mail campaign
- ❯❯ Create a website
- ❯❯ Write a newsletter
- ❯❯ Hold seminars
- ❯❯ Host client events
- ❯❯ Attend trade shows
- ❯❯ Try e-mail marketing
- ❯❯ Form strategic alliances
- ❯❯ Do some cold calling
- ❯❯ Get involved in a charitable or civic organization
- ❯❯ Take out some advertising
- ❯❯ Write a book
- ❯❯ Join a professional association for those in your target market

>> Use referral letters
>> Start networking
>> Write a column
>> Host a radio show
>> Join (or start) a leads club
>> Design a multimedia business card
>> Buy leads

Adding a new product or service specialty can have a dramatic effect on your business. Here are some products and services to research.

>> Separately managed accounts
>> Disability insurance
>> Health insurance
>> Mutual funds
>> Financial planning services
>> Hedge funds
>> Executive benefits
>> Life insurance
>> Annuities
>> College planning
>> Individual equities
>> Employee benefits
>> Pension plans
>> Retirement planning
>> Estate planning
>> Charitable giving
>> Exchange-traded funds
>> Living trusts
>> Initial public offerings (IPOs)
>> Business succession planning
>> Real estate investment trusts
>> Unit investment trusts
>> Closed-end funds
>> Commodities
>> Pre- and post-divorce planning
>> Business insurance
>> Financial planning for corporate employees
>> Fixed-income investments
>> International equities
>> Index funds

A third area for research is methods for managing your business. Here are a few ideas to investigate and consider implementing.

>> Hire an assistant
>> Implement a paperless office

>> Create partnerships with other professionals
>> Make a transition from a commission- to a fee-based practice
>> Become an independent financial adviser
>> Become an independent insurance agent
>> Write a business plan
>> Become certified as an independent registered investment adviser (RIA)
>> Become a niche company
>> Acquire other firms
>> Devise some exit strategies
>> Start using a contact management software program

Every organization—not just businesses—
needs one core competence: innovation.

—PETER DRUCKER

 **POP QUIZ**

1. *The 60-20-20 Rule is an excellent way to jump-start your business.* ☐ True ☐ False
2. *You should devote 20 percent of your time to re-educating yourself about your industry.* ☐ True ☐ False
3. *You should devote 20 percent of your time to harmless but practical jokes.* ☐ True ☐ False
4. *You can expand your business by simply making yourself better known.* ☐ True ☐ False

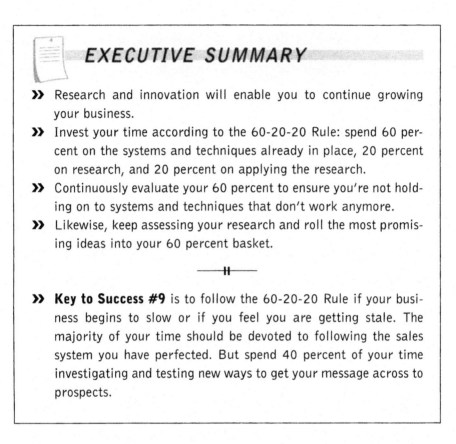

EXECUTIVE SUMMARY

» Research and innovation will enable you to continue growing your business.

» Invest your time according to the 60-20-20 Rule: spend 60 percent on the systems and techniques already in place, 20 percent on research, and 20 percent on applying the research.

» Continuously evaluate your 60 percent to ensure you're not holding on to systems and techniques that don't work anymore.

» Likewise, keep assessing your research and roll the most promising ideas into your 60 percent basket.

———‖———

» **Key to Success #9** is to follow the 60-20-20 Rule if your business begins to slow or if you feel you are getting stale. The majority of your time should be devoted to following the sales system you have perfected. But spend 40 percent of your time investigating and testing new ways to get your message across to prospects.

Automate Your
Sales Process

*The first rule of any technology used in a business is
that automation applied to an efficient operation will magnify
the efficiency. The second is that automation applied to an
inefficient operation will magnify the inefficiency.*

—BILL GATES

A LONG TIME AGO, BEFORE THERE WERE COMPUTERS, SALES-
people understood the importance of organizing leads and the
need to make sure they followed up with prospects in a timely fashion. Practically every professional salesperson used a powerful and
elegant system. Most people referred to it as the "card box."

The card box was single-handedly responsible for more sales
than any script or closing technique. It was treated with respect and
considered as valuable as gold, because it was in fact gold. Like the
wheel and the lever, the card box was simple, yet those who chose
to use it created a new world of organization.

The card box usually contained hundreds of three-by-five-inch
or five-by-eight-inch index cards. The cards were divided into two
major sections. The front section had tabs numbered one through
thirty-one, and the back section had tabs labeled January through
December.

Each card had prospect information on it. It contained, among
other things, contact information, such as the prospect's name,

address, and phone number. On each card, the salesperson kept a running history about what was said and when. All the information relevant to making the sale was kept on the cards, including product interests, past purchases, and others involved in making the decision. Personal information, such as birthdays, hobbies, family, and so on, was recorded on the cards.

Each day the salesperson would reach into the corresponding section of the card box. For example, if it were the fifteenth of the month, the salesperson would take all of the cards in tab number fifteen. These were the people who were to be called on that day. Some of the prospects would need to be called later, such as on the twentieth, in which case the card would be moved to the twentieth. Sometimes prospects would suggest calling back the following month. The card would then be moved to the appropriate month.

On the first day of each month, the salesperson would take out the cards for that month and begin calling. After each call, the card was moved ahead to the appropriate section and tab.

The beauty of the card box was that it assured that no prospect would fall through the cracks and every lead would be followed up in a timely fashion. Every prospect was immediately written up on a card with all the relevant data needed to close the sale.

The card box wasn't perfect, and there were lots of variations, depending on the salesperson, the products, and the selling process. But the bottom line was that the entire sales process and could be traced back on the card. The history of the sale, from the opening to the close, could be tracked.

The salesperson could also track sales activity. If there were thirty calls in the tab for that particular day and the salesperson had made all the calls, he knew there was probably adequate sales activity for the day. Problems such as a lack of leads, qualified prospects, or sales were glaring and tended to be addressed quickly.

This was before the information revolution and the computer age. Enter sales automation and contact management software. Literally overnight, the card box became a museum piece worthy of the Smithsonian, and it deserved to be. As good as the card box is, contact management software is even better. With this tool, you

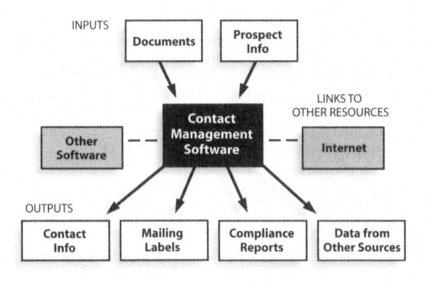

can record all of the relevant data on every prospect and client, keep records of every conversation, and get daily reminders of phone calls or sales activities that you need to implement, plus a whole lot more.

Contact management software offers myriad features and capabilities that are radical advancements over the card box. Thousands of prospects can be stored, and contact information and mailing labels can be printed out with a keystroke. The software programs interface with the Internet and other software programs, allow networking, and enable data from other sources to be downloaded easily and effortlessly. Documents can be stored and filed for easy access, and compliance reports can be generated with the click of a mouse.

All of these features offer you the capability to organize, track, file, and store every single piece of data relevant to every prospect and client. Automated contact management is the necessary tool to store the answers to all of the questions you ask. As you open the Johari Window and build relationships (see Key 11), you can store the information and have it right in front of you the next time you call.

—‖—

Sales automation is the card box on steroids. It is the single most important technological advance in selling. It is inexpensive to buy and easy to use. If you are serious about selling, contact management software is absolutely necessary. Without consistent, timely, and flawless follow-up, you will miss countless sales opportunities. With it, you will save endless amounts of your most valuable resource, close more sales, and feel confident that your sales process is 100 percent organized.

In the Resources section on page 189 is a list of quality contact management software programs for you to review. Many will allow you to download a demonstration version of the software to test for thirty days before buying.

▶▶ ACTION STEP
USE CONTACT MANAGEMENT TECHNOLOGY

If you are already using contact management software, congratulations! If you are not, get it today!

❓ POP QUIZ

How many financial professionals does it take to organize 1,000 sales leads?
   a. Four
   b. Ten
   c. None—the contact management software does it

EXECUTIVE SUMMARY

>> To be hugely successful you need to continue to cross-sell to your existing clients and approach them with new solutions to their financial problems.

>> Historically, financial products and services salespeople have used a simple but effective card box to remind them it's time to call a client. These card systems are time-consuming and difficult to search. For example, which of your clients don't have disability insurance? You can't answer that question using a card system.

>> Today's contact management software programs are inexpensive and easy to use and allow you to easily scan your clients for certain characteristics or needs.

———ǂǂ———

>> **Key to Success #10** is to automate your sales process. This means acquiring one of the many available contact management software programs, entering client information, and using the system to tell you when it's time to contact a client about his or her changing financial needs. Getting and staying organized is the #1 task for the productive salesperson.

KEY **11**

Open the Johari Window

There is no hope of joy except in human relationships.

—ANTOINE DE SAINT-EXUPÉRY

YOUR LONG-TERM SUCCESS IN TODAY'S FINANCIAL MARKET-place will be determined largely by your ability to create and grow relationships. Closing the sale, repeat business, and referrals all depend on your relationship-building skills. In fact, the quality of your life overall hinges on how well you establish and maintain relationships. Unfortunately, most people devote little time to studying this incredibly important process.

One of the most powerful models for understanding how to build productive relationships was discovered in the 1950s by two University of California psychologists, Joseph Luft and Harry Ingham. This model, applied to the sales process, can ensure more sales, more productive business relationships, and a higher client retention rate.

The model is called the Johari Window, a combination of the first names of the inventors. It describes the dynamics of relationships and answers the question, "What do I have to do to create effective and profitable relationships?"

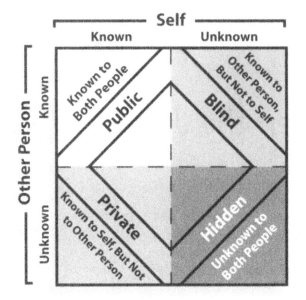

The Johari Window graphs information that is known and unknown between two people. This information includes attitudes, feelings, behavior, values, way of life, background, wants, interests, needs, and desires, as well as other factual information such as birthday, anniversary, and so forth.

The information that you know about yourself and that the other person knows about you is called the public quadrant, or open window. Public information can be basic, such as your name, your marital status, where you went to college, your hobbies, or your favorite sport. It can also include deeper and more personal information, such as your spiritual beliefs, dreams for the future, family concerns, or political views.

The range of information that resides in the public quadrant depends on a variety of factors, including the nature, quality, and length of the relationship. The size of the public quadrant depends entirely on whom the relationship is with. Generally, we share the most personal information with the people we are very close to.

The information that you know about yourself but that the other person doesn't know is called the private quadrant or window. The

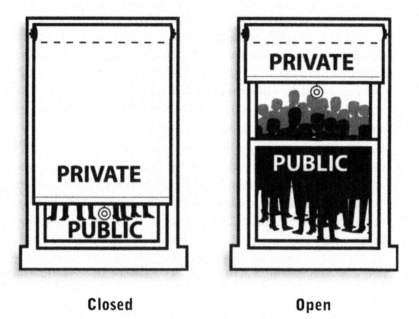

Closed   Open

private window is large in the beginning stages of a relationship. As a relationship grows and trust builds, information that began as private could enter the public quadrant. Information in the private quadrant might include your religious and political affiliations, personal medical problems, and long-term goals in life.

The information about yourself that is known to the other person but not to you is called the blind quadrant or window. For example, suppose you were sitting in a restaurant and you got a bit of food on your chin. The other person would know this, but you wouldn't.

Often in a marriage or close friendship one partner will say, "Oh, I never do such and such," and the other partner will drop his jaw in disbelief and say, "I can't believe you just said that! You *always* do such and such. Why, just the other day you...." Thus, the third quadrant represents personality traits or behaviors that you are unaware of.

The hidden quadrant or window includes information that neither person knows. It contains our hidden desires, undiscovered talents, and so on. For example, you might have the potential to be very good at skydiving, but there is an excellent chance you will never find out and that it will remain in the hidden quadrant.

In relationships that are unproductive or ineffective, the Johari Window is "closed." The public quadrant is small; the amount of information that is shared is limited. You know very little about the other person, and the other person knows very little about you. When you're meeting with a prospect, it's difficult, if not impossible, to make a sale with the Johari Window closed.

On the other hand, as you begin to gather information and get to know your prospect, you will open the Johari Window. This open window is characteristic of practically all productive relationships. Let's face it, you usually know a lot about the people with whom you have the best relationships. This applies to both your business and your personal relationships (see illustrations on the previous page).

The secret to creating relationships is to become an expert at opening the Johari Window. In order to open it, you must become masterful at soliciting information from the prospect. The more you know about your prospect, the more productive the relationship is likely to be. The faster you can do it, the better.

Initially, this might be personal information disclosed in the rapport-building stage. You ask nonthreatening questions to learn about the prospect's occupation, background, hobbies, and so on. As you move along in the sales cycle, you might be gathering information or fact-finding in order to determine the most applicable products for a prospect.

If you can find out what drives your prospects—what their needs, fears, and concerns are and what's important to them—you will be creating a relationship, as opposed to making a product pitch. You will begin to feel as if you know them and have more than a professional relationship. You may say, "They are not just my clients; they are my friends."

The best way to understand the dynamics of opening the Johari Window is to think back on a long-term personal relationship, such as a friendship or a marriage. Initially you knew very little about the other person, and she knew little about you. As time passed, you learned more about her, and, feeling more comfortable, you disclosed more information about yourself. Once you opened the window on yourself a bit wider, the other person felt even more comfortable, and in turn disclosed more information about herself. And on it goes.

Similarly, the way to encourage your prospect to share information is to share information about yourself. By disclosing appropriate information at the appropriate time, you will motivate your prospect to open the window even more.

For example, suppose you are conducting a meeting with a client and find out that he and his wife are expecting a second child. This might be the perfect moment to share your own experience by saying something like, "You know, when my wife, Joanne, became pregnant with Lila, our second child, I became concerned for our family's security. For my own peace of mind, I made some adjustments in our insurance plan. It helps me to sleep at night, and I feel better about my responsibilities as a father. How do you feel about taking a look at your current policy and developing a few scenarios to consider?"

Or perhaps you want to open a discussion on retirement planning. It is very helpful to understand your prospect's existing retirement plan. Opening the Johari Window would enable you to directly connect your services to your prospect's dreams. It would be appropriate in this instance for you to share information about your own retirement expectations. "Fred, you know Marilyn and I love to play golf, and we love to travel. One of our dreams for when I retire is to travel and play on the best golf courses all over the world. What are your retirement dreams?"

In both of the above examples, you are opening your Johari Window to your client. This creates an atmosphere of trust and motivates the other person to open up to you. The operative word is "appropriate." We have different criteria for what is appropriate in each relationship in our lives. We will share certain information with one friend but not another, other information with our spouse but not a friend, and so on.

There are no hard rules regarding what to share and when. Initially, you must use logic. As the relationship unfolds and mutual trust evolves, you share more and more information. In the context of a professional relationship with a client, the mistake most financial professionals make is failing to open the Johari Window far enough, rather than opening it too far. The reasons for this include the failure to see the importance of building relationships, a lack of understanding of how to build relationships, and a lack of comfort with the process itself.

Knowing what and who is important to your prospects and clients is not just an interesting interpersonal social exercise. It is essential if you want to expand your professional relationship. How can you help your clients plan for retirement if you don't know what their retirement dreams are? How can you design an effective life insurance plan if you don't know whom they love and care about? How can you address wealth transfer if you are not familiar with the people, causes, and organizations your client is committed to?

To attempt to serve your clients' needs professionally and at the highest level, you must delicately and discreetly explore their underlying feelings, values, and goals. This knowledge of the other person is what creates the unique value in the relationship.

In this respect, the impersonal nature of the Internet has served financial professionals well by highlighting the defining difference they can make in helping individuals purchase the financial products and services that best suit their goals. Many people become even more confused by the plethora of information out there. They then realize that they need an adviser who knows and understands them, someone who has opened the Johari Window.

▶▶ ACTION STEP

TAKE A LOOK OUT THE WINDOW

Here's an exercise to help you develop your skills in opening the Johari Window.

Step one. During the course of a day, from the minute you wake up until you go to sleep, make an effort to open the Johari Window with every person you interact with. This includes people with whom you have personal relationships (such as your spouse and children), business relationships, and incidental relationships. Observe how the quality of your relationships improves when you ask questions, listen, and disclose information with each interaction.

Every time you come in contact with someone, you have an opportunity to open the Johari Window. And every time you open the Johari Window, you are building a productive relationship. As the quality of your relationships improves, so does your ability to enlist support, get things done, and create business opportunities.

Open the Johari Window with your delivery person, your administrative assistant, your compliance officer, your manager, your partner, your dry cleaner, your gas station attendant, your waiter, and your dentist. You get the idea.

Step two. Spend one day consciously keeping the window closed. Don't solicit information, and don't disclose any information.

Step three. Compare the experience of a "closed day" with an "open day."

Here's what most people experience when they do this exercise. First, you will notice the difference in how people respond to you. When you open the Johari Window, you are engaging people. Therefore, they will become more responsive to you. When you do not open the window, you will not feel a connection to the people you are interacting with, even if you are courteous and agreeable.

Second, your interactions will have more depth, and you will enjoy your interactions more. The waiter or the delivery person will probably respond to you in a more positive manner after you open the window. In general, you will find your day more satisfying.

Third, you will discover it is relatively easy to initiate and build relationships by applying the Johari Window model. Every relationship during the course of your day will become more developed. It is almost impossible not to expand your relationships when you open the window.

Fourth, and most important on a professional level, you will build relationships that will result in new business opportunities. For example, you could sit down on an airplane for a transcontinental flight and open the Johari Window with the person sitting in the next seat, asking questions, listening, and disclosing information. You discover he is unhappy with his current financial adviser. The result: a follow-up meeting in your office and a new client.

Or suppose you are an insurance agent, and you bring your clothes to the dry cleaner. You take some time to open the window and discover the owner's wife has just had a baby. You discuss the need for college planning. As a result, you create and implement a college plan for his new child.

You should also apply this principle to existing relationships. Build relationships with your current clients, and you will uncover new business opportunities. The more you know about your clients, the better you can serve them. For example, let's say you open the window with a client by telling her that you've been concerned about your father's health lately. During the ensuing conversation, she opens up a bit more than in past meetings, and you discover that she feel her parents are quite frail. You discuss the likelihood of her parents' needing medical care as they age. The result: you sell a long-term-care policy.

As you can see, opening the Johari Window builds trust and a relationship. Rather than the prospect feeling as though he is being interrogated, which is a danger in the sales situation, he now feels as though he is in a normal conversation, in which the other person (that's you) is sharing experiences, concerns, and opinions. That is a much more comfortable place for him to be, and so this kind of conversation is far more likely to garner you the valuable information you need than a straight line of questioning, no matter how reassuringly phrased. What's more, you'll be building a relationship based on mutual trust, which is the best way to have lots of clients rather than lots of prospects.

Therefore, refine your questions, improve your listening skills, and become comfortable with allowing others to know appropriate information about yourself. You will find that you close far more sales and make more money when you open the Johari Window.

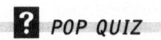

POP QUIZ

Which of the following sales elements are affected when you open the Johari Window?

a. Qualifying
b. Rapport-building
c. Establishing trust
d. Determining needs
e. Identifying benefits
f. Handling objections
g. Closing
h. All of the above

EXECUTIVE SUMMARY

>> The Johari Window is a model for understanding how to build productive relationships. Applied to the sales process, it can help you close more sales and increase your client retention rate.

>> When you open the window of information on yourself, prospects will in turn open up to you, giving you more information about themselves and helping you develop profitable long-term relationships.

>> Sharing some personal information about yourself helps the sales process seem more like a conversation and less like an interrogation.

———‖———

>> The more information you share in the public window, the more your clients will get to know, respect, and trust you, and the more they will want to do business with you. That is **Key to Success #11.**

Market Yourself as the Expert

In those days he was wiser than he is now;
he used frequently to take my advice.

—WINSTON CHURCHILL

THE MORE YOU LEARN ABOUT FINANCIAL PRODUCTS AND MAR-
kets, the more you want to talk about them and tell people everything you know. Guess what? Nobody cares.

Most people do not care about hedge funds, whole life versus
variable insurance, balanced index funds, and separately managed
accounts. *You* care, and that's great and as it should be. The government regulatory commissions care. The product managers care. But
the truth is, the people to whom you want to sell these products do
not care about the specifics.

On the other hand, the more you know and care about the things
your prospects *do* care about, the easier it is to make the sale.
Consider that prospective clients are, above all, solution driven. They
have a problem or a need but no solution. You have the solution, and
your expertise is to match the need to the product or service, not
simply to sell. Matching needs is called consultative selling.

What do your prospects care about? They care about taking control of their future with a well-designed financial plan. They care

about being able to achieve retirement dreams. They care about making prudent investment decisions. They care about leaving a huge percentage of their estate to the people they love rather than to Uncle Sam. They care about leaving society and the world a meaningful legacy after they are gone. They care about the peace of mind of knowing their families will be safe and secure if the primary breadwinner dies suddenly.

Your prospects care about a lot of things. They just don't care about your products and services, because everyone has the same things to sell. But if you sell yourself as a financial expert first, you will be viewed as a consultant and remove the stigma associated with being a salesperson. Sell the concept of yourself as a solution provider. The products are merely the means to an end.

The need to become an expert has been amplified by the evolution of a new era in the financial industry. The industry is no longer compartmentalized, and the consumer now has virtually unlimited access to financial products and services. Insurance agents are selling investment products, investment advisers are selling insurance, and banks and CPAs are selling financial products. You can buy just about anything from a wide variety of professionals. And, of course, you can buy most financial products without speaking to anyone at all, via the Internet.

—H—

In this new era, the public has unprecedented access to information. What the consumer desperately needs is expertise and guidance in sorting through this onslaught of information. By establishing yourself as a financial expert, you will have what people want. It's a heck of a lot easier to make money by having what people want than by selling people what you have.

The things your prospects care about fall into broad categories in which you can establish your expertise. These categories include the following:

>> Financial planning
>> Asset allocation

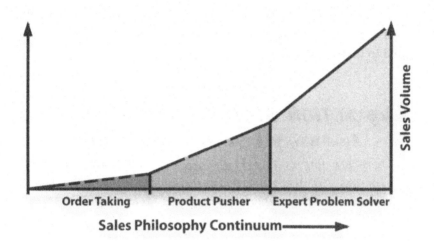

Sales Philosophy Continuum ⟶

>> Retirement planning
>> Estate planning
>> Charitable giving
>> Employee benefits
>> College funding
>> Tax planning
>> Trusts
>> Risk management
>> Long-term health care

A true expert sells intellectual property—ideas—and you should do the same with your expertise. This concept could be applied in areas such as financial planning and estate planning. As your practice becomes more consultative in approach, you might want to carry the idea of selling your expertise through to your compensation and formalize the relationship with your prospect before doing any work. This shift is often necessary, because once you begin to position yourself more as an expert and a solution provider than as a salesperson, you may very well find that your prospects become more sophisticated, with needs that are more complex. Therefore, you will also find that you cannot afford to do the work without some form of fee-based compensation. In any case, avoid sharing your solutions without a commitment and an agreement of some kind to do business.

▶▶ ACTION STEP

EIGHT WAYS TO ESTABLISH YOURSELF AS AN EXPERT

There are lots of things you can do to demonstrate your expertise. Try the strategies below to begin gaining public recognition as an expert. Adapt these ideas to your market and to the specific problems you specialize in solving for your prospects.

Write a column or articles. Contact your local newspapers, magazines, newsletters, and other publications and identify the people who review article ideas. Most publications are continually seeking articles that are relevant to their readership. In many cases, you can get to know the contact person and brainstorm article ideas with her.

Articles and columns are particularly valuable because you can hand out reprints at seminars, mail them to clients and prospects, and submit them to other media outlets when you are seeking additional opportunities. Having an article in print solidifies your reputation and demonstrates your expertise in a very tangible way. You have the best chance of getting exposure in the media if your idea has a great title and a hook to a current event or trend.

Get quoted or interviewed in the media. The best way to accomplish this is to send out story ideas on current financial issues to print and broadcast reporters. (Make sure you check with your compliance office first.) If a reporter you contact decides to do an article based on your idea, there is a good chance that he will call you for a quote or an interview.

One example of a financial story idea is the changing law on estate taxation and what one can do to minimize exposure for the next generation. Another example that was hot in the winter of 2004 was what to do if you owned shares in a scandal-ridden mutual fund. Keep your eyes open for good story ideas in the financial press and consumer financial magazines, on financial websites, and from professional financial associations. Send out story ideas that connect to current events and trends as you come up with them.

Media referral programs are another extremely valuable resource. These typically are sponsored by professional associations such as the Financial Planning Association, as well as the financial credentialing organizations listed in the Resources section beginning on page 191. When you sign up for a media referral program, you will be asked to list the topics on which you are an expert. Then, when the media contact the group for information on those topics, the group will refer the reporters to you. (Make sure that before giving comments, you've cleared them through your firm's public relations or compliance officer.)

Send newsworthy press releases to the media. For example, suppose your firm is involved in noteworthy charity work, or you have received an award or been recognized in some way. Send out a short press release on it, and one of the local media outlets just might want to interview you or write about it. If you are speaking or conducting a seminar, be sure to send a press release to upcoming events departments of the local media two to three weeks in advance. If your seminar is free, you may get a free mention in the local events listings.

Host your own show. While this may sound implausible, it really isn't. Cable television in many areas of the country offers ordinary people the opportunity to do a weekly show. Although the viewing audience is usually small, that doesn't matter, because you can leverage the opportunity. You can easily get tapes of the show, use them to create your own media kit, and pursue other publicity opportunities.

Likewise, explore opportunities to host a radio show on a local station. Radio shows have helped many people establish themselves as experts, attract desirable clients, and promote upcoming seminars. If you can find a sponsor or even sponsor the show yourself, you will probably be able to get airtime. Here, too, you'll want to visit with your firm's compliance department or representative because they will be interested in your commentary and the content you intend to cover.

Seek Internet exposure. There is a whole world of media exposure available on the Internet. One simple but effective method is to e-mail comments and story ideas to financial websites. Make yourself available for speaking engagements. Getting in front of groups of people will literally and figuratively position you as the expert. Whether you conduct your own seminars or speak at other organizations' meetings, you will automatically be seen as an authority on the subject at hand.

Speaking to groups that comprise your target market is particularly effective. Rather than trying to sell them, play the role of the expert providing solutions to their financial problems or concerns. Remember, it's all about pain relief and problem solving.

Write and publish a book. This is a daunting challenge, but it can be done. You can write it yourself or get help from a professor of the appropriate subject at your local college. If you want someone to write a book for you, type ''ghost writer'' into any Internet search engine and you will come up with hundreds of very competitively priced services. You can do the same type of search for self-publishing services.

Producing a book takes time and money, but the result is an incredibly powerful tool for establishing yourself as an expert. In our achievement-driven culture, having a book under your belt is one of the most effective ways of establishing your credibility.

Prepare a brochure about yourself, highlighting media exposure, speaking engagements, and recognition by trade associations. Make sure prospective customers see your professional brochure, which can only help them form an ''expert'' opinion about you.

The more information from credible sources you can accumulate about yourself, the better. Prepare a scrapbook for your waiting room that prospective clients can glance through to see that you are an expert recognized by the media and professional associations. Cover your office walls with pictures of yourself making speeches, receiving awards, being interviewed on TV, or with money managers associated with your product inventory. Prospects will see these demonstrations of your proficiency and come to think of you as an expert. There are so many simple, reinforcing ways such as these to position yourself as an expert —a provider of solutions to prospects' problems.

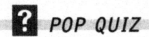 POP QUIZ

Which of the following are effective ways to prove you're an expert?
a. Shout it from the rooftops.
b. Prepare a press kit of your articles and interviews.
c. Wear a button that says "Expert."
d. Host your own radio or TV show.
e. Write a book.

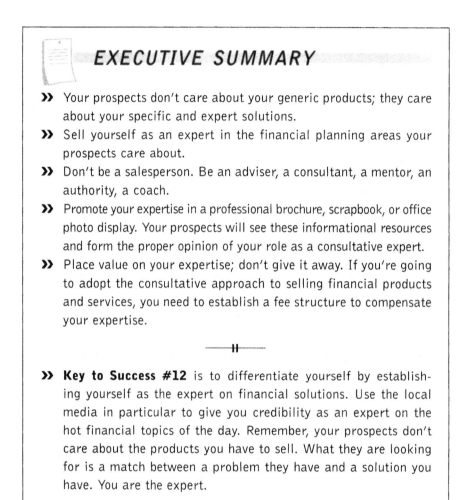

EXECUTIVE SUMMARY

» Your prospects don't care about your generic products; they care about your specific and expert solutions.

» Sell yourself as an expert in the financial planning areas your prospects care about.

» Don't be a salesperson. Be an adviser, a consultant, a mentor, an authority, a coach.

» Promote your expertise in a professional brochure, scrapbook, or office photo display. Your prospects will see these informational resources and form the proper opinion of your role as a consultative expert.

» Place value on your expertise; don't give it away. If you're going to adopt the consultative approach to selling financial products and services, you need to establish a fee structure to compensate your expertise.

———— ‖ ————

» **Key to Success #12** is to differentiate yourself by establishing yourself as the expert on financial solutions. Use the local media in particular to give you credibility as an expert on the hot financial topics of the day. Remember, your prospects don't care about the products you have to sell. What they are looking for is a match between a problem they have and a solution you have. You are the expert.

Generate New Business with Existing Clients

It's not the will to win, but the will to prepare *to win that makes the difference.*

—PAUL "BEAR" BRYANT

LOTS OF FINANCIAL PROFESSIONALS LIKE TO THINK ABOUT HOW much income they want in the coming year, yet most fail to capitalize on the most obvious and easiest source of new business: their existing clients. Many professionals have a variety of products at their disposal but overlook the opportunity to go back to the clients they already have and cross-sell more of those products to them. Therefore, you can give your income a real boost by engaging in a simple yet dynamic process: creating plans to do more business with every client.

There are lots of opportunities lying within every single client relationship. Do you expect your clients to come to you with new ideas for products you can sell them? That's very unlikely. It's your job to identify new opportunities and sell the products and services your clients need. It's your job to think ahead and be prepared to suggest additional ways you can serve them.

Unless you secure a new client through a referral, selling more products and services to existing clients is at least ten times easier than finding new clients. In most cases, substantial investments of time, effort, and resources are required to find new clients. Inertia is working against you. The distance between you and the new client is considerable.

Prospect <<<<<<<<<<<<<<<<<<<<<<<<<<<<<<<<<<<<<<<<<<<<<< New Client

INERTIA   High investment of time, energy, and resources

On the other hand, after you have successfully created a new client relationship, you develop momentum. Instead of fighting inertia, you move forward with new business opportunities quickly and easily. The momentum of the relationship means you need to invest very little time, energy, and resources. In many cases, successive sales to existing clients are more significant than the initial business.

Client → New Business → New Business → New Business → New Business

MOMENTUM   Low investment of time, energy, and resources

Create marketing plans for your existing clients as part of your annual business plan and implement them during the coming year. If you do, two-thirds of your income each year will come from your existing clients and one-third from new clients. If you are interested in increasing your income in the coming year, you'll find new business from existing clients the easiest to acquire and the business you can count on most.

Here's how you can generate more business with existing clients. Follow this simple, four-step process to boost your income significantly.

1. Know your client. If you have been conscientious about opening the Johari Window (see Key 11), have gathered the relevant financial data, and have filed all of this information in your contact management software, you should already know your client very well. Remember that you need to move beyond just the financial fact-finding. You should be familiar with your clients' lives, what and whom they care about, and their long- and short-term goals.

If you are a full-service financial adviser, you will have been diligent about this step throughout the process. It is impossible to responsibly write a financial plan without knowing this information. In addition, it is likely that you already conduct regular telephone and face-to-face meetings with your clients to update this information.

On the other hand, if you are more product-centered in your approach, you might need to integrate systems into your sales process that will enable you to know your clients better and to collect relevant client information. The most effective way to do this is to schedule regular meetings with your clients.

2. Analyze the information. Review each client one at a time. How often you do this will vary depending on your business model and the client. You probably know lots about certain clients and their upcoming needs and less about others. At the very least, you must analyze your clients' needs annually.

Essentially, you are looking for holes in their financial affairs. Regardless of your business model and the products and services

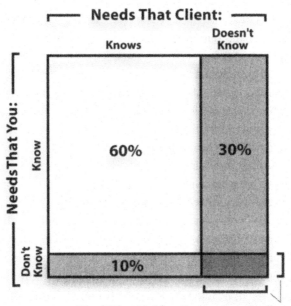

Areas of Sales Opportunity Based on Client Needs

you sell, there will be opportunities, either existing or arising in the future, that you could, should, and, in some cases, must address in the interest of serving your client.

Opportunities for the coming year fall into three categories: needs that both you and your client are aware of, needs that you can foresee but that your client doesn't, and needs that neither you nor your client can predict. For every dollar of additional compensation that you derive from your existing clients, 60 percent will be generated from the first group of needs, 30 percent from the second group, and 10 percent from the third.

3. Marry your products and services with your client's needs. This is the sacred dictum of selling in action: "Find a need and fill it." What products and services do you sell that will fill one or more of your client's current needs? How can you more effectively fulfill your mission as a financial professional? This is not about pushing products; it's all about being conscious of the undeniable fact that the client doesn't know what the client doesn't know.

It is your responsibility to inform, remind, and motivate action that is in a client's best interest. For example, let's say your client is a business owner who has purchased a lot of annuities from you. The business opportunities shouldn't end with that sale. The client might have other significant needs that should be addressed. She might need an estate plan or a benefit plan for her employees, or perhaps she has children or grandchildren for whom she would like to set up a college funding plan or trust.

Similarly, you might have a client who has purchased mutual funds from you. You know this individual needs life insurance. This is a product that you offer and that would be valuable for him to own. It would be wise to set up a meeting to discuss life insurance in more detail.

4. Implement your marketing plan for all of your clients, not just a few. It is very common for financial professionals to neglect exploring possibilities with all of their clients. This is a big mistake that must be avoided. By continuing to explore needs and expand relationships, you can build serious business with clients who currently are less significant. Ask yourself the question: What account, need, product, or service have we not talked about in the last twelve months? Chances are if you haven't talked with them about it, somebody else will. Your best clients are someone else's best prospects.

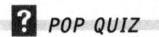

POP QUIZ

How much money do you leave on the table each year by not having a marketing plan for each client?

a. None
b. Very little
c. Some
d. More than I'd like to admit

EXECUTIVE SUMMARY

>> Your greatest opportunity for new business is existing clients.
>> It's a lot easier to sell to existing clients, because you can harness the momentum created by the relationship.
>> Evaluate your clients for needs you are not currently filling.
>> By exploring new possibilities with all your clients, not just a few, you can build serious business with those who currently are less significant.
>> Make calls, set appointments, and have fun closing the sales.

——||——

>> **Key to Success #13** is to prepare an annual marketing plan for each of your clients, identifying products and services you think the customer will appreciate but also leaving room for exploring financial products and services that neither of you have yet considered. Nearly 80 percent of your business will come from repeat customers, so "cultivate what you have in your own backyard." These clients already know you and respect you. They have experienced the added value that you have brought to your relationship. They know you are not just a salesperson. They know you take their financial vitality seriously. Then why not score with them first?

Master the Art
of Communication

Communicate unto the other guy that which you would want
him to communicate unto you if your positions were reversed.

—AARON GOLDMAN

THE FINANCIAL INDUSTRY CONTINUES TO OFFER THE OPPORTU-
nity to achieve the American Dream in all its glory. Unlimited
wealth is available to anyone, regardless of social position, background,
ethnicity, gender, religious affiliation, race, or economic status. Good
communication skills are the only prerequisite for success.

The selling process in the financial services industry is substantially different from that for other products. For example,
automobile salespeople rely on the test drive to create interest
and desire. Similarly, real estate agents can ask a few questions
about the buyer's criteria and then show the properties that fit.
However, to excel in selling financial products and services, the
financial adviser must employ more advanced communication
skills. Exceptional questioning, listening, and presenting skills
are the tools of the trade for the financial salesperson. The top
producers are those who have taken the time to master these three
deceptively simple activities.

You don't want a million answers as much as you want a few forever questions. The questions are diamonds you hold in the light.

—RICHARD BACH

Questioning is the most important communication skill and sales tool. All the answers to closing the sale reside in the questions you ask. Here are ten reasons questions are so important in the sales process.

1. Questions provide your prospect with the opportunity to feel important.
2. Questions uncover her needs and problems.
3. Questions reveal his pain and fears.
4. Questions qualify the prospect.
5. Questions build trust by keeping the focus on your prospect.
6. Questions identify objections.
7. Questions allow you to relax during the selling process.
8. Questions allow your prospect to relax by creating a conversational atmosphere.
9. Questions enable you to discover his values.
10. Questions allow you to take and keep control of the sales process.

If you want to improve your questioning skills, you need to know what you sound like during the sales process. With that in mind, take a look at the following six-step exercise. It will enable you to make a quantum leap in your selling ability.

▶▶ ACTION STEP

EVALUATE YOUR QUESTIONING SKILLS

1. Audiotape five sales conversations with prospects. (Naturally, ask for the prospects' permission before you do this.)
2. Listen to the tapes.
3. Time how long you speak and how long your prospect speaks.

4. Count the number of questions you use during each conversation.
5. Evaluate your performance based on the following criteria.

—Are you speaking about 20 to 30 percent of the time?

—If you find that you are speaking more than this, you must include more questions.

—What is the quality of your questions? Is there an underlying rationale for them? Do they all reveal valuable information? High-quality, targeted questions will decrease your selling time and increase your closing ratio. Every question should have an intention. You must know why you asked it.

—Are your key questions scripted, or do you shoot from the hip? Although there is nothing wrong with customizing, adapting, and personalizing your approach, remember that professionals employ powerful, well-thought-out questions during the selling process. These are questions that they have down pat and can rely on over and over again.

6. Ask your sales manager, coach, mentor, or someone you trust and respect to listen to the tapes and give you feedback.

One often hears the remark "He talks too much," but when did anyone last hear the criticism "He listens too much"?

——NORMAN AUGUSTINE

Listening is the most overlooked skill of all great salespeople. Selling is 80 percent listening and 20 percent talking. If you talk more than 20 percent of the time, you are probably blowing the sale. If you were to sketch the proportion of time you should spend on each step in the sales process, ideally it would look like the diagram below.

```
|----------------------------------------------------------|--------------|-|
       Questioning and Listening                   Presenting        Close
                                                   Handling Objection
```

When you listen, you are satisfying a need that every human being has. This need is as basic and powerful as the need for air, water, and food. It is a need that is never sated, and you, as a financial professional, have an unlimited supply to offer. When you listen, you are providing your prospect with respect and dignity.

All those great questions we just talked about mean nothing if you do not listen well. The answers to the questions discussed in the previous section will provide you with all of the information you need to close the sale. Listening is the heart and soul of every enduring relationship we have in our lives, both professional and personal.

Here are three guidelines you should consider to improve your listening skills. Even great listeners can improve by adhering more closely to these ideas.

First, follow the three immutable rules of effective listening:
1. Shut up.
2. Don't talk.
3. Keep quiet.

Second, pay close attention to five nonverbal factors that physically and psychologically show the prospect you are listening.
1. *Physical position.* Are you in the ideal location and close enough to listen? In every conversation, there is an ideal distance from the person speaking, one that is the most comfortable for both of you. This distance can vary slightly depending on the closeness of the relationship. But if you are too far away, your ability to listen will decrease drastically.
2. *Environment.* Is the environment free from distractions and quiet enough?
3. *Body language.* Is your body square with your prospect and leaning forward slightly? This communicates your interest in and attention to what he is saying.
4. *Eye contact.* Are you making good eye contact with your prospect?
5. *Prompts and cues.* Do you use prompts such as "hmm," "uh huh," and "ahh" to acknowledge what is being said and encourage the prospect to continue?

Third, employ active listening skills. Active listening proves to the prospect that her words and feelings have been heard and understood. In order to listen actively, you must set aside your own agenda.

Active listening by definition means you are doing something during the listening process. You are paraphrasing the content and feelings that you hear and feeding them back to the prospect. Phrases such as "What I hear you saying is," "I guess what you are saying is," and "In other words" are good ways to lead into this feedback.

For example, the prospect might tell you, "I think investing in equities right now is rather risky. Perhaps it will level out soon." You could use active listening to say, "I guess what you are saying is you don't feel comfortable investing in a market that appears to be quite volatile right now."

Active listening skills require ongoing paraphrasing and feedback. Generally, such feedback will occur every three to five minutes during a conversation. There is no hard-and-fast rule, but you should definitely paraphrase whenever the person concludes an important point, thought, or feeling.

It is also essential to recognize the importance of the underlying feelings that drive many of your prospect's financial decisions. Financial data, such as assets, liabilities, and current investments, can easily be collected in a fact finder. Numbers aren't open to a lot of interpretation. Your challenge is to actively listen for the feelings, values, and personal goals that will enable you to serve the true needs of the individual.

For instance, if you are involved in estate planning, you need to know whom and what the individual cares about. Estate planning can be technically complicated, so it is essential for the individual to know you are perfectly clear on his priorities and goals. The individual will trust your plan only if he knows you know the underlying objectives.

Active listening requires patience and practice to use and master, but it makes your prospect feel heard and respected. It is one of the most powerful techniques you can use to make him feel important.

—‖—

The words you use to present your products and services must be based on the answers to the questions you asked the prospect. Your job is to provide solutions to the prospect's problems and needs, which you have uncovered with your questions.

Remember that sales are made for emotional reasons and justified with logic. Your suggestions must appeal to the emotions and passions of the prospect. Paint pictures with your words. Find creative ways to engage and involve your prospect's emotions. If you want your presentation to sell to the emotions, include the following appeals:

» Stories
» Metaphors
» Analogies
» Humor
» Illustrations
» Visuals

Your ability to touch your prospect's emotions will also be greatly affected by how you sound. All studies in persuasive communication support the idea that the words themselves are less important than how you sound.

The tone, volume, and clarity of your voice, as well as the rate of speed at which you speak, will have a profound effect on your ability to influence the person across the table. It is very easy to determine the most effective presentation style: simply mirror and match the vocal mannerisms of the person to whom you are speaking. If he talks fast, talk fast. If he's loud, talk loudly. Also, match the tone of his voice. If he talks in a soft and soothing manner, you should, too.

Mirroring and matching is a natural process that most people adopt unconsciously to communicate optimally. For example, most people will automatically slow down to match an older person's cadences. Similarly, if you are speaking to a child, there is a tendency to raise your pitch to sound closer to hers.

When your intention is to influence or persuade, listen to how your prospect sounds, and then mirror and match. Your message is more likely to be heard when you sound like the person to whom you are speaking. Plus, you will feel more in tune with your prospect.

POP QUIZ

If you want to become a top producer, ask brilliant questions. Do you currently employ precise questions that assist you in achieving specific selling objectives? For each question below that you answer yes, rate your consistency and prowess on a scale of one to ten.

1. *Do you use questions to arouse interest?*   ☐ Yes   ☐ No
2. *Do you use questions to help build personal rapport?*
☐ Yes   ☐ No
3. *Do you use questions to qualify your prospect?*
☐ Yes   ☐ No
4. *Do you use questions to reveal past experiences with your particular product?*   ☐ Yes   ☐ No
5. *Do you use questions that identify pain?*   ☐ Yes   ☐ No
6. *Do you use questions to identify what is most important to your prospect about your product or service?*
☐ Yes   ☐ No
7. *Do you use questions to identify objections?*
☐ Yes   ☐ No
8. *Do you use questions to create yes answers?*
☐ Yes   ☐ No
9. *Do you use questions to separate yourself from your competition?*   ☐ Yes   ☐ No
10. *Do you use closing or "call to action" questions?*
☐ Yes   ☐ No

If you scored 100, you are probably not being entirely truthful. If you scored between 80 and 100, you're doing a great job. Your greatest opportunity for improvement might be in refining your questions.

If you scored between 50 and 80, you're using questions moderately well, but you probably have serious weak spots. Include more questions, and you will close more sales.

If you scored below 50, you are telling and not selling. Very few people can survive in the financial industry with a rating of that level, but you can increase your closing ratio 100 percent with question-based selling.

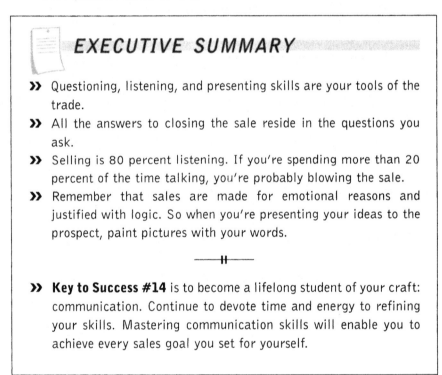

EXECUTIVE SUMMARY

» Questioning, listening, and presenting skills are your tools of the trade.

» All the answers to closing the sale reside in the questions you ask.

» Selling is 80 percent listening. If you're spending more than 20 percent of the time talking, you're probably blowing the sale.

» Remember that sales are made for emotional reasons and justified with logic. So when you're presenting your ideas to the prospect, paint pictures with your words.

———— ‖ ————

» **Key to Success #14** is to become a lifelong student of your craft: communication. Continue to devote time and energy to refining your skills. Mastering communication skills will enable you to achieve every sales goal you set for yourself.

KEY 15

Demand Objections

Salesmanship starts when the customer says no.

—GEORGE O. BOULE, JR.

THE ONLY OBJECTIONS YOU CANNOT OVERCOME ARE THOSE THAT are unspoken. Objections are actually buying signals. They prove your prospect is interested but has concerns or needs more information before making a commitment to move ahead. Therefore, instead of dreading a prospect's objections, look forward to them. That's what the excitement of selling is all about.

In fact, demand, even "program," objections. Become an objection hound. Selling doesn't begin until you hear your prospect's concerns. Your ability to handle his objections is the defining difference between selling and order-taking.

There are only three situations in which your prospect will have no objections at all. Let's look at these situations first before discussing strategies for addressing the objections that do come up.

In the first instance, you have done an excellent job throughout the selling process: creating rapport, building a relationship, establishing trust, asking smart questions, listening, identifying the prospect's problem, and presenting products and services that will provide him with solutions and value. In this scenario, your prospect probably asked a variety of questions, requested more information, and voiced his concerns throughout the selling process, and you addressed all of these issues successfully. In this scenario, your sales approach clicked in just the right way.

The second type of situation occurs when you haven't qualified the prospect properly, for whatever reason. Seminars are a good example of this pitfall. When you hold financial seminars to market yourself, it may not be as easy to qualify the people who attend, because you may use direct mail marketing to fill the seminar seats. It's not unusual for people who attend financial seminars to be more interested in the free dinner than they are in the offer of a consultation. As a result, when you have a call to action at the end of the seminar, it is quite common for people not to offer specific objections to your request for an appointment. Instead, they might provide you with the old standby fogger, "I'll get back to you."

The reason these individuals don't have any objections is they never had an interest in your topic or your products and services in the first place. Your presentation may have been on target, but these members of the audience were not. Seminar attendees who are genuinely interested, by contrast, will ask for more information about the free consultation.

The third situation occurs when you've done a poor job of qualifying the prospect financially. In a typical scenario, you present your investment product to someone who seems genuinely interested, asks astute questions, and appears ready to move ahead with the sale. He offers no objections, but when you ask him for the order, you are shocked and dismayed to learn he has a mere $1,000 to invest. This happens to be $99,000 shy of your minimum investment. If you frequently find yourself in this situation, you need to rethink your methods of qualifying your prospects. Your prospects must be qualified, interested, and financially capable in order to make the sale work.

It's important to understand these no-objection situations, because you may very well run into them, for better (situation #1) or worse (situations #2 and #3). Any prospect who doesn't fall into one of the three previous categories is bound to have hidden fears or concerns that he won't bring up until you ask for a commitment or request an action. Therefore, if you fail to seek objections, uncover the prospect's hidden concerns, and provide the additional information that he needs to feel comfortable, you will also fail to close the sale.

—H—

During the selling process, there is a moment of tension. Both you and the prospect know it's coming. It happens when you ask for a commitment. At this important juncture, it's easy to become hesitant, allow the prospect to take control, and let the conversation drift. This moment often occurs when you ask for an action to proceed with the sale.

Most people at this point are seriously considering moving ahead and are not quite sure how to do so, or they are trying to say no and do not know how to do that. This is the moment when you need to take control and find out how they are feeling.

Here's the best way to take control and secure the information you need to make the sale. Ask the prospect this simple question: "Right now, are you leaning more positively toward my recommendations, or more negatively?" It doesn't matter how he answers this question. Either way, the answer will help establish that there are obstacles standing in the way of closing the sale.

You see, if the answer is, "I'm leaning more positively," the prospect will be helping you to make the sale, by reiterating out loud the primary benefits of your proposal. Then you can encourage him by asking, "So what's stopping you from moving ahead?" The answer will be something like, "I'd like to go ahead, but...". At this point, he'll probably list two or three things that are worrying him. Boom! You have hit the pay dirt you are looking for: objections. Now you can answer his objections one by one and move toward closing the sale.

If, conversely, your prospect says, "I'm leaning negatively," and you ask, "*What* is it that is causing you to lean negatively?", you will hit the same pay dirt. Your prospect will provide you with the objections that, up to this point, he has hidden from you. You can continue with the sale by providing the information he needs to make the decision, assuming logic will outweigh emotion, as we have previously discussed.

In both instances, you will achieve your objective—getting the information you need to move ahead with the sale. No matter what the problem is, you need to know the issues your prospects are struggling with. For example, let's say you are discussing the creation of a retirement plan, and you ask which way the prospect is leaning. He may say something like, "I'm leaning more positively, because I really am concerned about creating a secure retirement plan, one that I can count on."

This answer reveals the key to making the sale and what you need to emphasize to move forward—your prospect's need to be reassured that the plan is truly secure and that the money will be there for him when he retires. Now you have a framework for handling any remaining resistance.

If, on the other hand, the prospect replies negatively and says that he isn't comfortable with what you are proposing, you can use this answer to discover exactly what is bothering him. Suppose the prospect says, "I really don't like the idea of paying commissions. I'd rather buy no-load funds and eliminate the commissions." This is an objection to which you can provide a variety of answers, but at least you will know what the real issue is for him. Discovering exactly what is bothering the prospect is critical to closing the sale.

Although you should always aim to have the prospect tell you exactly what is on his mind, keep in mind that there are a limited number of objections to any sales proposal. Your job as a professional is to be prepared to address every one of them. It is very likely your prospect will say one thing and mean another. In addition to the reasons the prospect tells you up front, you must also address the underlying objections that he might not be verbalizing. When you attempt to close the sale and hear an objection, much of what the prospect says merely conceals the way he feels.

For instance, one of the most common objections is, "I need to think about it." Although that might sound reasonable enough, there is often an unspoken objection, namely, "I'm not convinced." In this case, there is a good chance you failed to develop trust with the prospect from the outset. This is probably the result of failing to ask the right questions and listen (see Key 14 for more guidance on these issues). You might need more time to develop the prospect's trust in you, perhaps meeting with him a few more times to develop the trust in a natural and organic way.

An appropriate analogy for this particular issue is going to the doctor. If you have an ailment and the doctor makes a suggestion, you take her advice. You take her advice because you trust her insights, diagnosis of the problem, and experience in providing effective solutions. Trust eliminates the need to argue or question the doctor's suggestion.

Another common objection when you are attempting to close a sale is, "I have to check with my lawyer, accountant, investment adviser, partner," or whomever. For many people, this is a necessary step. This objection therefore becomes a detail that must be attended to in order for you to make the sale. Your job in this situation is to move forward by establishing a plan and a concrete time frame. Thus, the reply to this might be something like, "I realize it is very difficult to absorb all this information, and in fact, it wouldn't be prudent to make any decisions without your accountant. Perhaps you could set up a conference call for next week. Why don't you call me back on Thursday with a few possible days and times? We can firm up the conference call when you call me back."

—‖—

Know the truth and it will set you free to make the sale. Take your time when the prospect fogs you with a stall that masks the real reason for not proceeding. It's easy to understand the hesitancy associated with making decisions, especially when they involve financial matters that can have far-reaching and dramatic effects on economic security and well-being, but don't mistake the spoken reason for the unspoken.

Equally important, don't dismiss the spoken objection as unimportant. You must proceed with a discovery process and provide the prospect with the reassurance and information needed to make him feel comfortable with taking the action you are suggesting.

The most powerful way to deal with the spoken objections you will continually encounter is to "front with the objection." In other words, voice your prospect's objection for him early in the sales process, and then provide a solution.

For example, if the objection you regularly encounter is "I'd like to think about it," you could respond, "I understand making decisions regarding your financial future can be difficult, and there is a lot to think about. So before we complete our meeting today, I'd like to find out what specific information you need to think about or know. That way I can present it at our next meeting. I'm just interested as to what exactly you have to think about."

It is important to be tactful and professional, but as the title of this key states, you must demand the objection. You need the objection to close the sale, but you also need to know why the client is resisting taking action in order to better prepare your tactics and answers when confronted with similar situations in the future.

The art of successfully handling objections is a lot like war: victory is often achieved before the first shot has been fired. Plan your sale up front and address probable objections early in the selling process, and you will eliminate the need to handle them later.

Here are five guidelines for successfully handling objections.

1. Listen carefully to the objection. Even though you may have heard the objections a thousand times before, you must allow the prospect to voice his needs, concerns, and fears. Make sure you understand what lies behind the objection: fear, threatened self-esteem, lack of financial resources, and so on.

2. Never argue. If you allow the prospect's objection to degenerate into an argument, you will almost always lose the argument and the sale. Any goodwill you have earned will be lost if you argue with the prospect.

3. Acknowledge. If you seek to diminish or dismiss the objection, you are showing disrespect for the prospect. The objection may or may not be totally unfounded, but in any case, remember it is based on personal feelings that are real and troubling to the prospect. Deny those feelings and you will be denied the sale. Instead, you must confirm the importance of what he is saying. You must be sincere in this effort.

4. Completely expose the objection. Use questions to get objections completely out in the open. Allow prospects to elaborate on the basis for their objections, as well as the unspoken fears that are underneath them. Show interest and ask questions in a curious, rather than impatient, manner. Here are some good, productive questions to ask to get at the objections:

>> "What exactly is stopping you from taking action right now?
>> "What is the basis for your fears?"
>> "What information would be useful to you right now to help you make a decision?"
>> "If I get back to you in a week, what will have changed?"
>> "If it weren't for [this], would there be any other reason keeping you from getting started?"

5. Respond with benefits. As you respond to objections, reinforce the benefits of your product or service. Your response might sound something like this: "I understand your concern about the fees. Can you see how the tax benefits this plan will provide you will outweigh the fees associated with it and make this an extremely profitable opportunity?"

One of the most powerful and elegant methods for putting the above guidelines into practice is the "feel, felt, found" technique. After the prospect reveals an objection, tell him, "I know how you feel." This shows you have listened and understood. Then continue, "Other people have felt the same way." The second statement acknowledges the importance of what he or she is feeling and lends it legitimacy. Now for your third statement: "And what they have found is (fill in the benefits of taking action)." This provides your prospect with the logical justification for moving ahead with the sale.

▶▶ ACTION STEP
PREPARE YOUR RESPONSES

List every objection you encounter during the sales process and create a log of responses to each of them, based on the above guidelines. If you continually refine and improve the quality of your responses, you'll increase your sales exponentially.

? POP QUIZ

Objections are:
 a. A pain in the backside
 b. Terrifying
 c. A reflection of your sales acumen
 d. Your passport to closing the sale

EXECUTIVE SUMMARY

» Seek out objections. They prove your prospect is interested but just needs some more information or reassurance from you.

» Overcome objections by voicing your prospect's likely reservations early in the sales process, and provide a solution or address the issue in some way before it has even been brought up by the prospect.

» Prepare a response to every objection you encounter. That will enable you to put your prospect's fears to rest more easily so you can more quickly close the sale.

» Build your prospect's trust in you. Trust is the objection terminator.

——— ‖ ———

» **Key to Success #15** is to always anticipate objections to your proposal, to flush out the objections as you sense them during your presentation, and to have answers or solutions that allow the prospective buyer to say yes.

Always Be Closing

That you may be strong, be a craftsman in speech,
for the strength of one is the tongue, and
the speech of one is mightier than all the fighting.

—PTAHHOTEP, C. 3000 B.C.

THE PRIMARY ADAGE IN SELLING HAS BEEN, AND ALWAYS WILL be, ABC: Always Be Closing. This is the fundamental strategic philosophy of the systemized and formalized approach to selling that began in the mid-twentieth century.

Unfortunately, most people identify this philosophy with the negative stereotype of a salesperson: pushy, aggressive, manipulative, and offensive in one way or another. This association is unfortunate, because properly understood and applied, this strategy is the ticket to creating massive sales success.

Long-term success that is characterized by clients, not customers, must be an ethically guided process of persuading someone to take action that produces positive results for both people. In addition, the process needs to feel good for both people if you want to maximize your professional satisfaction. In the financial industry, doing the right thing leads to much more than good karma and an absence of compliance problems. It leads to an incredibly good living.

Selling based on integrity requires eliminating tricky closing gimmicks. Closing should not be based on a technique you apply at the end. Closing should permeate every single moment of the selling process. Closing begins the second an individual qualifies as a prospect. Closing is an attitude you maintain throughout the selling process. It is your goal, your driving force.

You are closing when you believe 100 percent in what you do and what you sell. You are closing by exuding a passion for what you sell. It can't be repeated too often: sales are made for emotional reasons and justified with logic.

You are closing when you keep your word, walk your talk, and behave in a thoroughly professional manner. You are closing when you build rapport and make the sale an interactive process with the client. A relaxed atmosphere and a conversational format create the optimal environment for presenting your products and services.

You are closing when you ask intelligent questions to identify the specific ways your products or services will contribute to the lives of your prospects. You are closing when you listen, giving prospects the respect and dignity they want and expect. You are closing when you present expert solutions to the specific needs and concerns of your prospects. You are closing when you focus on building trust in the relationship. When trust is present, your advice and suggestions are readily taken. Trust is a key to successful closing. It reduces the selling cycle considerably, allowing you to take on more clients and business.

You are closing when you are uncovering the values and life goals that are meaningful to the prospect. Understanding what's important to your prospect will help you create an emotional connection and a more meaningful relationship.

You are closing the sale when you deliver more value to the relationship than just the financial product or service. Adding value—through expertise, in particular—is one of the secrets to standing out in a crowded marketplace. And you are also closing when you carefully acknowledge the prospect's need for clarification or more information.

Yes, you are beginning to close the sale the moment you open it. It is up to you to maintain the closing attitude and reflect it in everything you do and everything you say during the selling process.

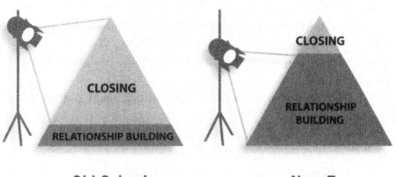

Old School   **New Era**

When your selling process is relationship-centered, much less time is spent actually asking for the order. Because the prospect has already been sold, there is no pressure or need for elaborate closing techniques. Asking for the order is more relaxed, because most of your time and energy is invested in building the relationship. This is the exact opposite of old-school selling, where not much time or energy was invested in building the relationship and lots of time was spent pushing the sale to a close. In reality, the modern salesperson who closes from the beginning and takes on the expert role rarely has to ask for the business. The prospect wants to say yes!

This does not mean you do not need effective scripts for calling to action. But because your selling process is relationship-centered, you have laid the groundwork for closing the sale with the assumptive close. Because you can provide the solutions and benefits the prospect is seeking, you are assuming the sale.

Assumptive closes are simple. You might say something like "Based on what you've said, I think we should (take the next action step) to move ahead," or "Let's get you on board," or "Sounds like we've got a good fit. Why don't we get the process going right now?"

The assumptive close is a specific call to action to the client. The call to action is not assertive; it is simply direct, when the timing is right. And if you have been closing since the beginning, the prospect will not be surprised when you ask for a commitment.

If you are not sure whether your prospect is ready to move ahead, or if you want to move a little slower, you can use a trial close. The difference between a trial close and a full close is a trial close asks questions that will reveal feelings or opinions, whereas a full close asks for a decision.

Here are nine effective trial closes you can adapt and use immediately:

1. "What other questions or concerns would you like to discuss before making a decision?"
2. "Is there anything else you need to know before you make a decision?"
3. "What are your thoughts about...?"
4. "How do you feel about...?"
5. "Are you comfortable with...?"
6. "What do you feel is the best way to proceed?"
7. "Is there anything that would prevent you from moving forward at this time?"
8. "Can you see how this plan...?"
9. "Have we covered everything you wanted to discuss today?"

It's important to recognize that most people have difficulty making decisions, especially about financial matters. That's just human nature. Therefore, you need to understand your prospect's problem and empathize. Assuming your products and services are important and beneficial, it is your responsibility to prepare scripts that will motivate the prospect to take action. If you don't, you lose, the prospect loses, your company loses, and our economy loses.

A few classic strategies for gaining agreement are worth their weight in gold. It will be worth your time to learn and embrace them. Since you will always be closing, you can integrate them in a variety of places during the selling process.

The alternate of choice. This is a question with two possible answers, both of which will confirm your prospect is moving ahead. The alternate of choice can be useful in a variety of situations where an intermediate action step is required. For example: "We've discussed two ideas. Would you prefer Mutual Fund 'A' or Mutual Fund

'B'? or "Sounds like we should set up another appointment. Would early next week work for you, or would you rather make it later in the week?" Or "I set appointments on Tuesdays and Thursdays. Which would work better for you and your wife?" Or "Would you like to come by my office, or would it be more convenient for me to visit you at home?"

The urgency close. It is often useful to provide the prospect with an immediate incentive, a reason to take action now. For example: "We would like to thank you for coming to tonight's seminar. To show our appreciation to you for attending, we are offering a free review of your current (insurance plan, investment portfolio, and so on). In order to be eligible, you must sign up tonight before you leave." Or "The current rates are excellent. They are based upon... Right now it is possible to lock them in. To do so we need to..."

The take-away close. This is one of the most powerful closes in selling. It is based on a basic and predictable human behavior: everybody wants what they can't have.

It's important to remember this close is effective only if the prospect is sincerely interested in your product or service, and you have taken the time to ask questions, listen, and build the relationship. Also, always mention the benefit of your product or service before you take it away.

Never be afraid to take the offer away. In most cases, the prospect will move toward you when you do, and if he doesn't, no worries: You can always put it back on the table. Here are some examples.

» "We've talked about how a sound financial plan can provide you with a sense of security, knowing you are taking control of your financial future. This seemed to be something of real value to you. But maybe my plan is not a good fit for you."

» "I know you love your family, and we've got the right programs that will help you to protect them in the event of the unforeseen. But maybe you and your family are more comfortable not addressing this issue. In that case, we should probably end the discussion right now."

Then there's the telephone take-away. It should be used only after you've developed rapport, had a good conversation, and established a relationship. If, after all this, you've left a few telephone messages and not received a call back, it's time to take it away.

>> "I've left you a couple of messages—I thought we had a great conversation, and that's why I've tried to get back to you. At this point I'm not going to call you again. If you do want to speak again or just to let me know my plan's not right for you, I'd love to hear from you. If I don't hear from you, then I wish you all the best, and good luck."

Probably the most important lesson in closing was taught by one of the pioneers in sales training and an absolute master of the art and science of selling. His name was J. Douglas Edwards. These fourteen words are as precious today as they were more than fifty years ago, when he would scream them at the top of his lungs at financial professionals: "Whenever you ask a closing question, shut up. The first person who speaks loses!"

Follow this advice whenever you ask a closing question. You will be amazed at how keeping your mouth shut will produce the best results you could ever wish for. You will either get exactly the response you are looking for, or you will uncover issues or objections that you need to address in order to make the sale.

▶▶ ACTION STEP
SYSTEMATIZE YOUR CLOSING PROCESS

If you have clients right now, you already have calls to action that work. More than likely, they are simple and direct. List your last five major sales. Then write down the trial closes or full closes you used for them. What worked the most smoothly? There is always room for improvement. Look for ways you can amend, refine, or revise your closing process.

Self-Evaluation

Sometimes financial professionals can feel conflicted about closing the sale. It can happen at the beginning of your career, after it matures, or intermittently under certain conditions.

There are a variety of reasons why you might experience emotional discomfort about closing. These include your discomfort with asking others for something; your preoccupation with the need to make the sale; your failure to focus on the value and benefit of your product or service; your lack of belief in the product; your fear of rejection; your unfavorable view of selling; low self-esteem; and maybe the fact that you never got to the point of establishing yourself as a solution expert. To get a handle on your discomfort, answer the following self-evaluation questions.

1. Do I feel any uncomfortable emotions when I ask the client for a decision or action?
2. Do I always focus on how I'm helping someone to allay my fears about asking for the business?
3. Do I sometimes fail to focus on the value I bring to the lives of my prospects and clients?
4. Do I sometimes feel or project too much pressure during the closing process?
5. Do I sometimes forget that I deserve to be highly compensated when I create high value and financial solutions?
6. Do I forget that I am an expert at what I do, a trained professional who takes on the immense responsibility of the financial security of my clients?

If you answer yes to any of these questions, you need to reread this chapter and evaluate how well you follow the ABC dictum: Always Be Closing. Identify things you can do during the selling process to become more comfortable with closing the sale.

POP QUIZ

See if you can correctly identify the elements of a good closing routine.

1. *The close starts the selling process.*   ☐ True   ☐ False
2. *The client knows you are going to ask for the business, so go ahead and ask.*   ☐ True   ☐ False
3. *Sales fail because the client isn't quite ready; this is when the trial close makes sense.*   ☐ True   ☐ False
4. *The best closers never have to ask for the business; the client already wants to say yes.*   ☐ True   ☐ False

---

EXECUTIVE SUMMARY

》 You begin closing the sale when you open it.

》 Closing is more than an event: it is an attitude.

》 Assume you will get the business if you have established a mutually profitable relationship.

》 The trial-close question asks for opinions and feelings. The full close asks for action.

》 "Whenever you ask a closing question, shut up. The first person who speaks loses."

——‖——

》 **Key to Success #16** is to begin the sale with a closing attitude. Everything you say and do during the selling process should lead to the close. If you are good, the client will recognize your expertise and the match between his problem and your solution, and he will trust you. When this happens, the close is automatic. It will happen every time.

Be Your Own
Sales Manager

Men who do things without being told draw the most wages.

—EDWIN H. STUART

THERE IS A VERY GOOD CHANCE THAT YOU DO NOT HAVE SALES managers breathing down your neck, watching your every move. If you are independent, you certainly don't have one, and if you're a member of a large organization, your sales manager probably plays a minor role in your day-to-day activities.

Weak or improperly trained sales managers contribute very little to your bottom line. In fact, they can de-motivate you with a heavy-handed, insensitive, or micromanaging style. It's safe to say you are better off without this kind of manager. Great sales managers, on the other hand, spend their time training, coaching, and motivating you to achieve higher levels of success. A great sales manager can provide inspiration when you are feeling low and can provide a sobering voice of reason when you mistakenly start to become a legend in your own mind.

Regardless of whether you actually have a sales manager, you must become your *own* sales manager. You must take responsibility for your own professional development and seek strategies and techniques for improving your sales results.

The first secret to becoming your own sales manager is to maintain "beginner's mind." Beginner's mind is an attitude of openness and receptivity. It allows for endless possibilities and many right answers to the questions and problems that arise in your professional life. Beginner's mind allows you to bring a fresh perspective to what you do every day.

By the way, beginner's mind is not only the secret to professional improvement; it is also the secret to staying young. Have you ever noticed how feeling alive and engaged in life is connected to this attitude of curiosity and learning that beginner's mind embraces? The times that you felt most vital and energized were probably when you were in school, learning your business, learning a craft, learning a hobby or sport, exploring new places, discovering new parts of yourself, or opening yourself up to a new relationship. It is essential to continually approach selling with a beginner's mind. Not only will you feel better, you'll also be more successful.

Beginner's mind will lead you through the four stages of learning. The first stage is called *unconscious incompetence*. You just don't know how to do something, and to make matters worse, you might not even know you don't. The second stage is *conscious incompetence* — that is, you *know* you don't know how to do it. The third stage is *conscious competence,* in which you know how to do something and consciously apply certain techniques to achieve results. The final and fourth state is mastery: *unconscious competence,* where you know how to do it and, what's more, you don't even have to think about it.

It is impossible to become unconsciously competent in every single aspect of the selling process. It just is. This is a humbling truth, and it provides you with the opportunity to keep learning and educating yourself. High achievers are never content with the status quo and continually seek to improve. That's why they are high achievers.

Your training must not begin and end with this book. Seek out other sales books, audio and video learning programs, and seminars that can provide you with advanced training. One of the most valuable techniques for improving your performance level is to enlist the services of a coach. Top-performing athletes, singers, dancers, and musicians recognize the power of coaching. Hiring a coach is a reflection of greatness, not weakness. So go ahead and hire a sales coach. The dividends of working with one will far exceed the investment.

—‖—

It's also up to you to motivate yourself. No sales manager or motivational speaker can motivate you. These people are valuable in your life and can inspire you, but they cannot motivate you to take action. Motivation is something that originates from within.

In order to be motivated, your desire for getting up in the morning and making money and having a great career must exceed your desire to stay in bed or do nothing. Making more money is not a matter of willpower. It's a matter of want power.

Motivation is simple to understand. Here's what will motivate you:

>> Your desire to be recognized by others
>> Your need to feel the satisfaction associated with achievement
>> Your family
>> Your aspiration to make the world better

If you want to motivate yourself, you must maintain your connection to your internal source of motivation. Don't judge it or evaluate it. What's important is your daily connection to the rewards of your efforts.

As your own sales manager, you must also monitor, measure, and manage your sales activity. Your income for the year is the direct result of the activity you initiate each day. The correlation between activity and results is the mathematics of sales success. It's easiest to visualize this relationship as a funnel. Sales activity goes in at the top in the form of calls. These could be telephone calls, face-to-face interviews, whatever. Of these calls, there will be a certain percentage of contacts. Of these contacts, some will qualify as prospects and enter the sales process, and from this group, you will ultimately close some sales and obtain clients and new business opportunities.

The numbers vary based on your prospecting method or sales process, but the product results can be predicted based upon activity. Here are a few examples. The formula for cold calling might look like this:

250 call attempts (dials) = 20 contacts = 5 prospects
= 1 new client

The formula for face-to-face calling might be something like this:

15 calls (doors entered) = 5 contacts = 3 prospects = 1 new client

For seminar selling, it might be:

2,000 calls (pieces mailed) = 25 participants = 10 appointments
= 4 new clients

If you want to know how much activity you need to achieve your sales goals, you need to work your numbers backwards. First, divide your annual sales goal by the average amount of profit you expect from each client. The result is the number of clients you need to achieve your annual sales goal. Based on your particular sales and marketing strategies, it is easy to calculate how many calls you must initiate to achieve your sales goal. For example, if the incremental sales goal is $100,000 and your average income per client is $2,000, then 100,000 divided by $2,000 equals 50 new clients. In this example, the formula for sales success is as follows:

50 calls per week = 10 contacts = 5 appointments with
qualified prospects = 1 new client per week

It doesn't matter whether you have a sales manager or not; you must keep an ongoing record of your sales activity. It will enable you to project future results. Numbers don't lie. You can't manage what you don't measure.

▶▶ *ACTION STEP*

CALCULATE YOUR SALES ACTIVITY GOALS

You've probably guessed it. This one is pretty darn obvious. It's also critical for your success. Let's do the mathematics of sales success based on your particular business model.

Step one. Write down your sales goal for the year: business from existing clients and business from new clients.

Step two. Calculate the number of *existing* clients and how much sales and profit you can expect from each one.

Step three. Calculate the number of *new* clients you need to reach the balance of your sales goal using the formula above.

Step four. Calculate your sales activity per day with existing and new customers: how many calls to existing clients, and how many prospecting calls.

Step five. Achieve your activity goals each day. Keep a daily record of your success. If your pace drops off for a week or two, you need to recalculate your activity if you want to maintain the same sales goal.

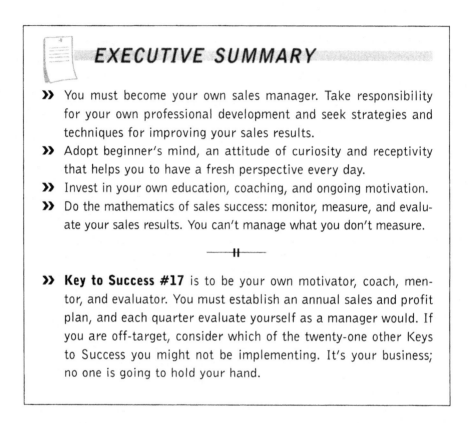

EXECUTIVE SUMMARY

» You must become your own sales manager. Take responsibility for your own professional development and seek strategies and techniques for improving your sales results.

» Adopt beginner's mind, an attitude of curiosity and receptivity that helps you to have a fresh perspective every day.

» Invest in your own education, coaching, and ongoing motivation.

» Do the mathematics of sales success: monitor, measure, and evaluate your sales results. You can't manage what you don't measure.

———— ♯ ————

» **Key to Success #17** is to be your own motivator, coach, mentor, and evaluator. You must establish an annual sales and profit plan, and each quarter evaluate yourself as a manager would. If you are off-target, consider which of the twenty-one other Keys to Success you might not be implementing. It's your business; no one is going to hold your hand.

Cultivate Your Referrals

I've never been shy about asking for help.

—TED TURNER

R EFERRALS REPRESENT THE SINGLE MOST IMPORTANT STRAT-
egy for creating lucrative new business opportunities with the
least amount of effort. More than half of all financial business is
referral-based, and so is more than 80 percent of all high-net-worth
business. It is also the least understood and most underutilized strategy. To live long and prosper in the financial industry, you must
accelerate your referral generation.

When speaking of referral systems, it's just as important to recognize the activities that *don't* accelerate referrals as those that do.
Waiting for business is an activity that does not accelerate referrals.
In fact, waiting as an activity is an oxymoron. Do a decent job, wait
for the phone to ring, and you are bound to get some referrals, but
this will represent a mere fraction of your referral potential.

Most financial professionals are riddled with fear when it
comes to asking for referrals. They are afraid to offend, afraid to
disappoint, afraid to bother, afraid to lose an existing client, afraid
to appear greedy or needy, afraid of rejection, afraid to make the

client uncomfortable, and countless other nameless fears.

Too many financial advisers vainly attempt to use a "referral script" that looks and sounds terrific but ignores the fears that will inevitably freeze them from taking action. Although scripts can be very useful tools, progress begins with the truth. You can begin to accelerate your referrals by first being truthful with yourself about your feelings.

Aside from fear, guilt is the second reason financial professionals are reluctant to ask for referrals. Your best clients are the people most likely to give you valuable referrals. But in many cases, you fail to give these clients the attention they deserve, and that makes you hesitant to ask for their help. It's simple math. Let's say you have 100 clients. According to the Pareto Principle (described in Key 2), 20 of those clients provide you with 80 percent of your income. Therefore, if you allocated your time according to your sales returns, you would give your best clients four times as many hours as your poorest clients. If you don't allocate your time this way—and many people don't—then you may be giving your poorest clients as much time as your best clients.

Somewhere in the back of your mind, you know this is not right. Even worse, your best clients are often the easiest clients—those who demand the least attention—so you may actually end up giving them *less* time than you do your less desirable clients. This increases your guilt level even more.

To eliminate guilt you must immediately begin to allocate more time to your best clients. As soon as you do they will probably give you more referrals, and you will certainly feel much more comfortable asking for them. To create a flow of lucrative referrals, employ the following four strategies.

Strategy one: Do a great job. It is difficult for anyone to refer you to their colleagues or friends if you have failed to do a bang-up job for them. With that in mind, here are three important guidelines to follow. They might seem simple, but the majority of financial advisers do not get perfect scores in all of these areas.

» Your objective with every client is to create a raving fan.

» You must always keep your word about everything, all the time.

» You must always serve the best interest of the client.

Strategy two: Maintain first-class communication. The number-one client-satisfaction criterion is good communication. This is true regardless of your product, service, or clientele. This even holds true when portfolios have lost significant value. It doesn't seem logical, but feelings aren't ruled by logic. The most effective communication techniques include regularly scheduled telephone calls, face-to-face meetings, e-mails, and newsletters.

Imagine if you had simple contact systems that maintained continuous communication with your clients, particularly those who could provide you with high-quality referrals. If you already have these systems in place, you are aware of the effects of quality client communication.

Strategy three: Refer to get referrals. It's the simple law of karma. If you give, you will get. Or to paraphrase the Beatles, the referrals you take are equal to the referrals you make. They were talking about love, but it works the same way with referrals.

The best way to influence behavior is to model it. That means, for example, that you sit down with one of your small business owner clients and say, "Bill, I've been thinking about you, and I realized I know a lot of people who could be valuable to you and your business." Take out a piece of paper and start with the names of five people who might be good prospects for his business or profession. Then give him five names of vendors or contacts who might be useful to him. Finally, offer the names of five people who could be good contacts for him on a personal level: an excellent massage therapist, a printer, a babysitter for his daughter, and so on.

Then you should close with, "Bill, look over this list and let me know which of these people I can call for you in advance to let them know you will be calling. It would be my pleasure to call as many as you'd like."

You make yourself a referral magnet when you spend your days helping your clients with referrals. This works with all clients, regardless of their occupation. Retirees, widowers, seniors, executives—anyone who might be your client will value a good referral.

Keep your eyes and ears open for people who could be valuable referrals. Maintain an ongoing list of great people to whom you can refer your clients. Everyone is looking for a great computer repair person, plumber, decorator, painter, housecleaner, gardener, personal trainer, yoga teacher, caterer, or whatever. Refer to get referrals, and you will reduce your guilt substantially. You will experience the joy of referring resources, and your clients will seek to return your thoughtfulness by referring their friends and colleagues to you.

Strategy four: Create hot referrals, not cold leads. If someone offers you a name and telephone number, you must recognize this as a cold lead. You must maintain a "no cold leads" policy. When someone offers to give you the name of a referral, you must ask for an additional step. A name and telephone number with a directive to "tell him I said to call" is only slightly better than a cold call.

The script for turning this cold lead into a hot referral is to say, "Sue, thank you so much, but you know what would be really helpful? If you could give Sam a call and let him know that we spoke and that I will be giving him a call. It would make all the difference in the world if you could do that." Almost everyone who is willing to give you the name and phone number of a referral will be willing to make the call, if you ask. When you call after they have contacted the referral, the entire tone of the conversation will be deeply affected. Your phone call will be returned, and you will be received warmly.

▶▶ ACTION STEP 1

CONDUCT CLIENT APPRECIATION EVENTS

An important way to increase your referrals is to hold a client appreciation event. The client appreciation event is the most powerful referral strategy there is. By using this technique, top producers in the financial industry accelerate their referrals exponentially.

The client appreciation event is any social or educational event used to increase client communication and to let your clients know how much you value your relationship with them. But most important, it is the perfect way to overcome your referral fears. Regular client events will eliminate any remaining guilt you might have about asking your clients for referrals. Such events could be birthday parties for clients, picnics, barbecues, golf outings, spectator sport events, seminars, luncheons, or dinners. The easiest to pull off are luncheons and dinners.

First, identify your best clients. Second, invite them to the event and ask them to bring someone else who might enjoy it. Third, follow up with all your clients and referrals.

This is the perfect referral scenario. Not only are your clients making the referral call for you, they are bringing the referral to you live and in person. Getting introduced to the client face-to-face is the hottest referral of all. Regular client events will accelerate your referrals beyond your wildest dreams.

▶▶ ACTION STEP 2

SAMPLE WORDING FOR GENERATING REFERRALS

If you're still feeling anxious about asking clients for referrals, here's a fantastic script you can use to generate a referral or two any time you speak with a client. Deliver it at the end of the client meeting or telephone conversation. As with every script, you must customize it to the person with whom you are speaking, your relationship, and your products and services.

"Robert, considering everything that's happened in the market over the past few years, it's not unusual for people to be somewhat concerned or confused about their investments, maybe even disappointed. If you have a friend or a family member who is feeling this way or would like the reassurance of a second opinion on their investment portfolio, please have them call me, and I will arrange some time to give them some feedback.

"If you do refer someone to me for a review, I will conduct a fifty-minute evaluation of the person's current financial situation. At that point, I will be very satisfied to let him or her know they are in good shape, or I might uncover a few areas that need to be adjusted. Either way, I assure you it will be a worthwhile investment of their time."

If you are still uncomfortable with a direct approach, here's a postscript you can include at the end of a memo to a client. It's a completely painless way to generate referrals.

"P.S. As you probably know, my business continues to grow as a result of my satisfied clients. It means a lot to me to know I have earned the respect and confidence of clients who have referred their friends and family to me. If you know someone in your family, retiring from your company, among your colleagues, etc., who would benefit from speaking with me, please have them call me." (See the Sample Scripts section starting on page 201 in Resources, for another proven referral script.)

 **POP QUIZ**

1. *It takes the same amount of time to cultivate a new customer as it does to develop an existing one.*   ☐ True   ☐ False
2. *Good clients like giving referrals, especially to a provider they respect.*   ☐ True   ☐ False
3. *One quality referral is as good as one hundred cold leads.*
     ☐ True   ☐ False

EXECUTIVE SUMMARY

» To prosper in the financial industry, you must accelerate the number of referrals you get.

» Treat your clients like gold, because that's what they are—a gold mine of valuable referrals.

» Hold a client appreciation event for your best clients, and ask each one to bring someone else. Getting introduced face-to-face is the hottest referral you can have.

———— ‖ ————

» **Key to Success #18** is referrals. They take the least time to cultivate because you have instant credibility, and they generate the most business of any new customer.

KEY 19

Create Your
Compelling Vision

*By believing passionately in something that
still does not exist, we create it. The nonexistent
is whatever we have not sufficiently desired.*

—NIKOS KAZANTSAKIS

P RACTICALLY EVERY SUCCESSFUL MAJOR CORPORATION IN
America has a vision statement. Large organizations invest
considerable amounts of time and money clarifying and defining
their vision of what the future will be and what role their company
will play in it. The reason is simple: visioning plays a vital role in
creating the future.

Your vision is a powerful mental image of what you want to create
in the future. It is your blueprint of what you intend to achieve and
provides your business with the direction it needs to move forward.
Your vision is a picture of how you intend to manifest your business
mission and purpose.

In the beginning, most people who get licensed and enter the
financial industry share a common vision—to pay the rent and
make a living. Those who stay focused on their vision and are
committed manifest it. In the beginning, this vision is adequate
and worthwhile.

The problem arises when you fail to consciously revise your

147

vision. Many financial professionals do not take the time to go beyond the make-a-living vision. But as your business grows, it is crucial to reassess your goals and change your focus accordingly. Your marketing and sales efforts must become more targeted along with your business model. There is a good chance that your old vision has resulted in too many clients who are not highly profitable or as desirable as they could be.

In addition, as your business grows, it often becomes less efficient. Operations systems and staff that worked in the beginning no longer work as well. Your time is often squandered in non-income-producing activities. You might find yourself working harder without seeing appreciable increases in income.

Knowing what you know after a few years in the business, you will be able to recreate your vision or come up with a new one. The financial industry offers an unlimited number of opportunities. There are countless business models that you were probably not aware of when you first entered the business.

It's like going to the guidance counselor's office in junior high school. Your inexperience makes it impossible for you to make optimal career choices, because you don't know what the choices are. It is only after a few years in the financial industry that you become aware of the choices and capable of deciding the best direction in which to go. Your future is yours to create, but you must take control of the process.

Visioning is not some kind of out-there process. World-class athletes use mental imagery to achieve their peak performance. Many athletes talk about picturing how they see themselves performing before engaging in the activity. It is easy to understand how consciously holding a positive mental image can support the desired results.

Visioning is best understood as the process of imagining. Albert Einstein understood its importance. He said, "Your imagination is your preview of life's coming attractions." What you imagine and focus on is largely what you get in life. Your vision creates a mental blueprint of your future. The positive image you maintain will become an ongoing source of inspiration as you work toward manifesting your vision. Keep your eyes on the prize, and you are more likely to win it.

To be effective, your vision should be meaningful to you on a personal level; it should be a reflection of your desires and your dreams. If you work with others, share your vision, because it will align the members of your group and increase their sense of purpose in what they do every day. When all the individuals you work with are "seeing the future" together, teamwork occurs naturally, and with it an increased sense of commitment.

—‖—

Before you create your vision, you must identify and clarify your values. Values are principles, standards, qualities, and deeply held beliefs that are important, worthwhile, and desirable. The root of the word value is *valor,* which means strength. Values are the answer to the question "What's important to you?" Your values determine how you behave as you pursue your vision.

Values are deep and emotional and are a source of strength for manifesting your vision. When you walk and talk your values, your prospects and clients respond positively on an emotional level. Here's how Robert Haas, chairman and CEO of Levi Strauss, described his experience with the importance of values: "We've learned that the soft stuff and the hard stuff are becoming increasingly intertwined. A company's values—what it stands for, what its people believe in—are crucial to its competitive success. Indeed, values drive the business."

Therefore, it is important to identify your existing values and let them drive your business. This is very different from creating values as "shoulds." When values are used to create rules governing what should and should not be done, they become oppressive rather than energizing and motivating. Values replace rules.

Your values will describe how you act as a financial professional as you pursue your vision. If you clarify and communicate these values to the people you work with, including your strategic partners, your prospects, and your clients, they will have some guidelines for their expectations of you.

Here's a wonderful example of a vision that's not from the financial industry but fulfills many of the above requirements.

I have a dream that one day on the red hills of Georgia, the sons of former slaves and the sons of former slave owners will be able to sit down together at the table of brotherhood.

I have a dream that my four little children will one day live in a nation where they will not be judged by the color of their skin but by the content of their character.

I have a dream that one day down in Alabama... little black boys and black girls will be able to join hands with little white boys and white girls as sisters and brothers.

...We will be able to speed up that day when all of God's children, black men and white men, Jews and Gentiles, Protestants and Catholics, will be able to join hands and sing in the words of the old Negro spiritual, "Free at last! Free at last! Thank God Almighty, we are free at last!"

Dr. Martin Luther King Jr.'s "I Have a Dream" speech expressed his vision for the future. This is an example of how a vision can capture the heart and spirit. Dr. King created a vivid picture of the end result; he did not talk about the implementation plan.

Obviously, your vision will not have the same expansive, far-reaching social dimension, but if it can be equally clear and results oriented, it will be a powerful tool for energizing and motivating you as you grow your business. Below are a few examples specific to the financial industry:

» "I provide families with peace of mind. My life insurance products are a reflection of my love of family. I persevere in my pursuit to provide life insurance to every family that cares about its loved ones. I have fun every day. My compensation continues to grow each year because I care about my clients, and they care about me. I am recognized by both my clients and my colleagues as the epitome of professionalism."

» "We help small business owners manifest their retirement dreams. Safety and security is the number-one priority in our investment philosophy. We maintain ongoing communication with our clients to ensure that the products and services we offer are based on our clients' goals and what's important to them. Our clients feel like friends, continually praise our work, and are a pleasure to work with. We are so prosperous that we are free to select our clients."

» "We provide high-net-worth individuals with the opportunity to use their wealth to make the transition from success to significance. Our success in creating charitable-giving opportunities contributes to the satisfaction and well-being of our clients, our society, and the world. Our clients have complete trust in us because they know that we really care, and we generate a continuous flow of profitable referrals from other professionals because of the quality of our work."

» "I safeguard the wealth of my clients. My long-term-care products provide protection from the risk of financial loss and the degeneration of lifestyle caused by long-term health problems. My expertise and my ability to respond quickly to my clients create effortless marketing opportunities."

▶▶ ACTION STEP 1

CLARIFY YOUR VALUES

Your business will benefit if you take a few minutes to clarify the values you stand for. Here's how to do it in three easy steps.

Step one. Review the list of values below and place a check mark in the appropriate column: always important (AI), sometimes important (SI), or not important (NI). Feel free to add other values that are important to you to this list.

	AI	SI	NI
Achievement (successful completion of tasks, results)	☐	☐	☐
Advancement (desire to get ahead, ambition)	☐	☐	☐
Balance (giving proper attention to each area of life)	☐	☐	☐
Challenge (testing limits)	☐	☐	☐

	AI	**SI**	**NI**
Communication (open dialog and exchange of views)	☐	☐	☐
Community (sense of involvement with others)	☐	☐	☐
Competence (being effective at what you do)	☐	☐	☐
Contribution (desire to make a difference)	☐	☐	☐
Control (desire to be in charge)	☐	☐	☐
Cooperation (teamwork)	☐	☐	☐
Courage (standing up for what you believe in)	☐	☐	☐
Creativity (innovation, finding new ways to do things)	☐	☐	☐
Discipline (self-control)	☐	☐	☐
Environment (respect for Earth)	☐	☐	☐
Fairness (respecting others' rights)	☐	☐	☐
Fame (desire to be well-known)	☐	☐	☐
Friendship (caring and support)	☐	☐	☐
Fun (pleasure and enjoyment)	☐	☐	☐
Generosity (desire to offer money and time)	☐	☐	☐
Health (physical fitness, freedom from illness)	☐	☐	☐
Helping (taking care of others)	☐	☐	☐
Honesty (the importance of being truthful)	☐	☐	☐
Influence (desire to persuade others and shape ideas)	☐	☐	☐
Integrity (acting in a way that is consistent with your beliefs)	☐	☐	☐
Learning (growth, knowledge, and understanding)	☐	☐	☐
Loyalty (allegiance)	☐	☐	☐
Order (desire to create stability)	☐	☐	☐
Peace (nonviolent resolution of differences)	☐	☐	☐
Perseverance (completing tasks, persistence)	☐	☐	☐
Personal development (self-improvement, continual learning)	☐	☐	☐
Power (authority over people and situations)	☐	☐	☐
Prosperity (flourishing, being able to afford things)	☐	☐	☐
Prestige (rank, status)	☐	☐	☐

	AI	SI	NI
Quality (excellence, high standards)	☐	☐	☐
Recognition (acknowledgment from others)	☐	☐	☐
Responsibility (desire to be accountable)	☐	☐	☐
Security (desire to feel safe)	☐	☐	☐
Service (desire to improve society and assist others)	☐	☐	☐
Self-respect (pride in self and feeling worthy)	☐	☐	☐
Spirituality (relationship to higher purpose and divinity)	☐	☐	☐
Stability (predictability)	☐	☐	☐
Teamwork (cooperating with others for a common goal)	☐	☐	☐
Tolerance (respect for others)	☐	☐	☐
Tradition (respecting the past and customs)	☐	☐	☐
Wealth (prosperity and abundance)	☐	☐	☐
Wisdom (seeking an understanding of life)	☐	☐	☐

Step two. Review the values you identified as always important (AI). From that group, list your top ten personal values.

Step three. From those ten values, list the five that are the most important to you in your work and in how you conduct your business. Those are the values to include in your vision statement.

▶▶ ACTION STEP 2

CREATE YOUR BUSINESS VISION

The following four-step process will enable you to create and benefit from a compelling vision of your business.

Step one. Relax. Find some quiet time to allow yourself to be creative. Some people find that the time when they've just awakened or just before they go to bed is the perfect time. Or maybe the right moment happens when you're taking a walk or spending time in nature. The important thing is to set aside some time to do this.

Step two. Imagine and dream about what you want your business to look like. Albert Einstein recognized the power of imagination when he said, "Imagination is more powerful than knowledge. For knowledge is limited, whereas imagination embraces the entire world, stimulating progress, giving birth to evolution." Don't judge or edit your thoughts. Write down your thoughts and repeat the visioning process two or three times, if necessary.

Step three. Clarify and refine your vision. After you have thought about your vision and written down some ideas, refine them into three or four sentences, using the twenty questions below, to create a precise image of what you want to create in the future. Review the examples in this Key if you get stuck.

1. Does your vision describe the future?
2. Is your vision expressed in the present tense?
3. Does it reflect the real benefits of your product or service?
4. Will it last for some time to come?
5. Does it illustrate greatness?
6. Does your vision inspire you to pursue it?
7. Will your vision be inspiring to others?
8. Are your values included in your vision?
9. Are your behaviors expressed in your vision?
10. Is your vision a picture of the end result?
11. Is your vision a clear and specific picture of the future?
12. Is your vision challenging and a stretch to achieve?
13. Is your vision easy to understand?
14. Does it allow for unlimited growth?
15. Have you included your products and services?
16. Does your vision include your target market?
17. Does it include your mission or purpose? (For a discussion of mission, see Key 3.)
18. Are professional competencies described in your vision?
19. Have you avoided describing how you will make it happen?
20. Does your vision differentiate you from your competition?

Step four. Visualize your future often. Use your quiet time to do this. What you focus on is what you get. At least once a day, use your vision to energize and motivate yourself.

EXECUTIVE SUMMARY

» Your vision is a blueprint of what you intend to achieve and create for your business in the future.

» This vision gives your business the direction it needs to move forward.

» Before creating your vision, you must identify and clarify your values.

» Your vision statement is what you would like the world (your financial community) to look like when you have finished your life's work.

———⊢⊢———

» **Key to Success #19** is the basic dream of what you expect to be the outcomes of your professional life. It is a statement that you always keep in mind because it is a reflection of your personal values, and it gives life to your mission and business.

Close More Sales
with Scripting

A student plays the instrument, a musician plays the music,
but the master plays the audience.

—ANONYMOUS

ONE OF THE MOST POWERFUL ANALOGIES FOR SELLING IS acting. The actor's job is to convince and persuade an audience. A great actor is capable of getting an audience to feel a particular way and producing a predetermined result. The actor seeks to create an emotional state in the audience. The salesperson has the exact same objective. If you do an effective job, the prospect's emotional state will dispose him to buy your products or engage your services.

The tools of the actor and the salesperson are identical. They both depend on communication skills. The words and the way in which they are delivered determine the success of both the actor and the salesperson. However, although every actor knows it is impossible to achieve greatness without a great script, it is safe to say that not every salesperson understands this critical fact. If you intend to close sales consistently, you must understand what scripts really are, how to create them, and how to deliver Oscar-worthy performances every time you meet with a prospect.

It is important to understand what a script is and what it is not.

A script is not a presentation that you read. Most people would be very disappointed if they had to watch actors on the stage simply reading their lines to the audience. People who read sales scripts are not professionals. They are, in fact, clueless about how professionals use scripts.

Scripting provides professionals with a track on which to run, one that offers the highest probability for success. It provides structure for the selling process so that you can move the prospect along from the opening to the desired ending—the close. Scripts provide salespeople with "magic words," words that will help convince the prospect to buy your products and services.

Professional scripting consists of three components: memorized modules, flexibility, and personalization. The memorized modules provide the perfect words. Flexibility allows you to insert modules as needed. Personalization means you adapt the script to your style.

It's easy to see how these elements work to your benefit during the selling process. Obviously, when you find words that motivate and persuade, it would be a waste to discard them. Imagine if each successive group of actors took it upon themselves to rewrite the words of Shakespeare. You get the point.

Unlike an actor, you are in a dialog with your audience. Your questions are scripted, and you have a variety of scripted responses to choose from, depending on what is said. For example, if the prospect says your fees seem high, you will have the perfect prepared response to address this issue most effectively.

Instead of getting flustered, you might respond, "How would you compare my fees?" Based on how the prospect answers, you will have the opportunity to help him understand how reasonable or competitive your fees are. Obviously, there is no magic formula for closing every sale. There are, however, scripts with well-thought-out questions, answers, and presentations that will provide you with the best chance to close a sale. This is flexibility, the second element of professional scripting.

The third element of professional scripting is personalization. Here again, the world-class actor studies the script, makes subtle refinements, and adapts the words to take complete ownership of them. In fact, the great actor *becomes* the character, and we perceive the words to be the actor's own.

"Frankly, my dear, I don't give a damn."

"I coulda been a contenduh."

"You want the truth? You can't handle the truth!"

"Make my day."

"Hasta la vista, baby."

"I'm king of the world."

"Good morning, Vietnam!"

We identify those scripted words with particular characters, not the actors playing them, because the actors fused the words to the characters they portrayed. You, too, must personalize your script and fuse it to your delivery style.

Financial professionals fall into four categories regarding scripting. **One group uses scripts without being aware of it.** In fact, they say the same things again and again. Some of the scripts they use are excellent, and some are terrible. Because they don't realize the power of well-thought-out scripting, they don't take time to create, evaluate, and refine their scripts. Consequently, they miss lots of business opportunities.

The second group misunderstands scripting and refuses to use it. These individuals believe scripts are beneath them in some way. They think they are more professional if they do not have to resort to scripts. Unfortunately, they suffer the same fate as the first group: lots of missed opportunities.

The third group represents those who have strayed from the path. These individuals have had positive experiences with scripts, perhaps early in their careers, but as time went on, they stopped using the original script that worked well, for one reason or another. They continued to amend, revise, and improvise on the original script. In time, the original script was replaced with another, less effective script. These individuals found that their closing percentages went down, yet they failed to see the relationship between scripting and sales results. They continued to use the revised and weakened version of their original script.

The fourth group understands the power of scripting and uses scripts well. They are believers and know that professionalism requires preparation. They realize that being prepared with scripted questions and responses increases their potential for success exponentially. They are continually on the lookout for scripts that work. When they find them, they keep them on file for use when the occasion arises. They know the secret to using scripts successfully is to customize and personalize them.

—‖—

Scripts are no secret, nor are they a new wrinkle. It is impossible to be involved in sales without hearing about sales scripts and how to use them. Practically every sales manager alive extols the virtues of sales scripts, and yet there is a lot of resistance to using them.

A variety of industry-related trends have also contributed to a de-emphasizing of the need for scripts. With the huge surge in independent insurance and financial professionals, there is very little sales training of any kind. Even within national organizations, there is often much less sales training available than formerly. Many financial professionals working within banks and accounting practices receive no sales training, and when they do, there is little time devoted to scripting.

And there are those who view scripting with disdain. They maintain a somewhat elitist attitude that reflects the belief that the quality of their work and technical abilities eliminates the need for training and scripting. Unfortunately, today's competitive marketplace in the financial industry has created an unprecedented need for quality scripting and sales training as a whole. But if you're still wary of using scripts, the following eight misconceptions and truths should convince you.

Misconception 1: Scripts aren't natural, so they aren't worth using.

Truth: Scripts are words on a piece of paper. Of course they're not natural. But it's your job to make them sound that way. Professional scripts should never sound memorized, nor should they sound as if they are being read.

Misconception 2: Scripts don't allow for spontaneity.

Truth: Scripts will set you free. You don't have to worry about finding the right words every time you meet with a prospect. You are free to focus your attention on delivering the words in a dynamic fashion.

Misconception 3: Scripts are too structured.

Truth: Scripts provide the structure for success. They have the elements you need to get where you want to go. They give you the structure with which to navigate from opening to close. Is there anything admirable about wasting time or getting sidetracked in the selling process?

Misconception 4: Scripts can lead to boredom.

Truth: This might be true to some degree. So what? It is hardly a reason to refuse to adopt a strategy that will create the shortest line between you and new business opportunities.

Let's assume for a moment you have a script that completely bores you, but you knew would result in a $10,000 commission. Would you be willing to use it and be bored? It's a given that professionals in any field must repeat behaviors to produce results. You see, the question becomes, "Are you bored with success?" Or "Are you bored with results?" Focus on the results your script brings you, and you will be a lot less bored. Consistency is a defining characteristic of a professional. Scripts ensure consistency. Scripts also reduce your prep time.

Misconception 5: Scripts are things you read.

Truth: Scripts are things you learn and then deliver from memory (i.e., from the heart).

Misconception 6: Scripts are for beginners.

Truth: Scripts are for winners. Winners have experienced the power of scripts to get results and are motivated to continue using them.

Misconception 7: Scripts weaken delivery skills.

Truth: Scripts allow you to speak with confidence. Without confidence, there is no sale.

Misconception 8: Scripts make you listen less effectively.

Truth: Poor listening skills don't come from using scripts. They are a symptom of an ineffective salesperson. Listening, like questioning and presenting, is a selling skill that must be learned. Effective salespeople have studied and refined the three communication skills, as described in Key 14. How you listen isn't affected by using scripts; it is affected by your understanding of its importance in the sales process.

Now that you understand the power of a good script, you're ready to begin crafting your own. Follow these guidelines for preparing effective scripts:

» **Write down your scripts.** It is important to have your scripts on paper. You will create scripts that are truly brilliant, and you must be able to duplicate them. Don't depend solely on your memory for this important task. Your purpose for writing them down is not to read them; it is to have a record of them so you can use them again.

» **Script smart questions.** Your time is your currency. Smart scripted questions will save you time qualifying prospects, identifying needs, and closing the sale. Craft your questions well.

» **Use a modular design for your script.** Selling is a repetitive and somewhat predictable process. Create modules for opening, qualifying, creating involvement, probing, handling objections, and calling for action.

» **Be creative.** Don't be afraid to try new twists or turns in your script. You will recognize the "keepers" when you come upon them. When you discover a gem, be sure to write it down.

» **Evaluate by results.** Your criterion for a script is not how it sounds or how it makes you feel when you say it. There is only one valid way of judging the quality of a script: results. Ask yourself how many sales the script helps you close, and what effect it has on your prospect's emotional state. Are you getting the results you're looking for?

» **Craft your words carefully.** Use words that excite the senses —words that allow the prospects to see, hear, feel, smell, and touch the pain they will avoid or the benefits they will receive by buying your products and services.

» **Collaborate.** Discuss your script with others who sell similar products and services. Share your scripts with one another. You can add to or revise your own script based on others' proven track records. Also, you can go to the Sample Scripts section starting on page 201 in Resources, for a collection of powerful and effective scripts you can begin using today.

Delivery is even more important than the words you use. Script delivery consists of two parts: visual and vocal. The visual aspect is your clothes, grooming, eye contact, movement, posture, facial expression, and gestures. The vocal aspect is the volume, clarity, tone, and speed of your speech.

If you've got great scripts, you need to deliver them in a dynamic fashion. You must put passion, enthusiasm, and confidence into your delivery. But remember that your style should be congruent with who you are. The legendary producers in the financial industry have not always been the most charismatic. The top producers have almost always been the most authentic.

▶▶ *ACTION STEP 1*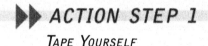

TAPE YOURSELF

One of the best ways to improve your script delivery is to videotape or audiotape yourself. By watching and listening to your delivery, you will make a quantum leap in your effectiveness.

The tape recorder will provide you with insights that even the best presentation coach would be challenged to impart to you. If you are delivering seminars, it is even more critical to tape yourself. Watching and listening to yourself is only slightly more pleasant than root-canal work, but the process pays back dividends that will last you for a lifetime.

▶▶ *ACTION STEP 2*

STAND AND DELIVER

Take an acting class. You will learn lots of techniques for making scripts come alive. You will also have a lot of fun.

In the same vein, take a singing class. It's not about appearing in Las Vegas or cutting an album. It's about how to use the sound of your voice to touch others. Singing a song is a perfect analogy for delivering a script. In both cases, you are using memorized words and an impassioned style to affect the emotions of the audience.

 **POP QUIZ**

What's black and white and red all over?
 a. An embarrassed zebra
 b. A newspaper
 c. The blood-soaked script of a telemarketer who's been mechanically reading a script over and over, all day long

---

EXECUTIVE SUMMARY

» To boost your closing ratio, you must understand what scripts really are, how to create them, and how to deliver Oscar-worthy performances to your prospects.

» Scripting helps structure the selling process and gives you the "magic words" for closing the sale.

» Scripts will set you free, because you'll have the right words every time you meet with a prospect.

» Professional scripting has three components: memorized modules, flexibility, and personalization.

» Improve your script delivery by videotaping it. By watching and listening to yourself, you'll make huge improvements.

» When you use scripts properly, the prospect is totally unaware that you're using one.

» **Key to Success #20** is to depend on scripts that are taken into active, flexible memory and personalized based on your sales approach and the selling situation.

Make Them Love You

Try not to become a man of success, but rather a man of value.

—ALBERT EINSTEIN

NOT TOO LONG AGO IN THE WORLD OF BUSINESS, SALES-people had a variety of product features they could use to differentiate themselves from the competition. Selling was based on a simple features-benefit model, and it worked very well. Lots of products offered features that provided significant advantages. Based on the features, closing the sale was a simple task. Or you could outsell the competition by offering products at a lower cost. Today, only Wal-Mart sells on price effectively.

That old world of selling is gone and will never return. Product designers possess an incredible amount of marketing intelligence, allowing them to pinpoint specific needs in the marketplace. Products are designed to meet the needs of the targeted market. This sophisticated product design capability is available to most manufacturers. When product features are matched to benefits for a target audience, competitive advantage has been created.

Product quality has gone through a similar evolution. Not long ago, high quality was the exception, not the rule. In the 1970s and early 1980s, Japanese manufacturers dominated sales in automobiles and electronics. Germans offered superior technical equipment. French wines were the first choice. Swiss watches were synonymous with quality. A select group dominated quality in various sectors.

Today the playing field has been leveled, not only in the world of manufactured products but also in the world of financial services. Because of the huge pool of shared information, the old world is gone forever. The financial industry has entered the age of commoditization. Practically all financial products have been reduced to the level of commodities. Competing on quality and unique selling features has become increasingly difficult.

Even if you can find a unique investment or insurance product today, it is usually only a matter of months before the competition comes up with something that is equally desirable or better. The financial marketplace is controlled by a Darwinian reality. Bad products do not survive very long.

As a financial professional, it's good to know you can feel pretty confident about the quality of what you are selling. Most of the products that are available for risk management or for wealth accumulation, preservation, or transfer are extremely competitive. Regardless of your business model, a vast array of these high-quality products is available.

The bad news is you are selling water. To the consumer, all of the products look exactly the same. It all looks like water. You may have a bell or whistle attached to your product, but product differentiation today is a thin thread to hang onto when you want to outsell the competition.

Competing on price or fee is also difficult. Most products and services are very competitively priced. A slightly lower or higher fee or commission will usually not be enough of a factor to win or lose a sale.

If you sell investment products and services based on historical performance, you are selling from weakness. The performance dream you are selling today can quickly become tomorrow's nightmare. When you sell products based on performance, you expose yourself to the risk of creating lots of one-time customers and few long-term client relationships. That's because the market can turn against you so quickly that you can't always respond fast enough to protect your clients' interests.

—⊪—

What to do? First, face the truth that your products and services are not enough of an advantage anymore, and then you can proceed to eliminate the competition and secure the competitive advantage. Most of the products in the same category look the same. It's no wonder your prospects are confused and frustrated when they must make a decision about whom to buy from.

Your best personal traits + client relationship → Adds value to the relationship → Exceeds client expectations → Increases referrals and client loyalty

The secret to having a true competitive edge in today's marketplace is to exceed client expectations. You must add value to the relationship that goes beyond the product or service you sell. You must be able to answer the question, "Assuming my product or service is a commodity, what is the added value I bring to this relationship?" In other words, ask yourself, "How can I make my clients love me"?

Before you jump in with the answer, "I give great service," keep in mind good service is not enough. Responding to calls in a timely fashion and providing good client communication no longer adds value to the relationship. Good service is considered a given. It doesn't add value or exceed client expectations.

You must exceed expectations twice: before the sale and after the sale. Before the sale, during the selling process, your objective should be to go beyond the sales ritual and become a person that your prospect would like to include in his life as a business partner.

For example, you could bring humor. Everyone likes to laugh. If your prospect has a good laugh and feels good every time he has contact with you, there is a good chance he will continue to offer you business opportunities. Given a choice, most people would rather have fun doing business.

Or maybe you can consistently affect your prospect positively and bring some sunshine with each contact. This will have a profound effect on how your prospect feels about you, add value to the relationship, and dramatically increase your chances of doing business. Good news about an opportunity is one form of sunshine.

Evaluate yourself and identify the value you can bring as a person to every relationship. Because you are selling yourself first, before your products and services, you must be clear on the traits and qualities you have that are most attractive to your prospect. Then, with each contact, you must sell yourself by highlighting these characteristics.

You can also sell yourself before the sale by keeping your eyes and ears open for creative ways to contribute to your prospect's life. For example, suppose she happens to mention something about wanting to learn how to play golf. This is an opportunity you can seize. You could give her a copy of a golf classic, such as *Harvey Penick's Little Red Book* or Ben Hogan's *Five Lessons: The Modern Fundamentals of Golf.*

Suppose you find out there has been a birth in your prospect's family. The few dollars you invest in sending a baby gift to his home will go a long way toward adding value to your relationship. Value in this case is sincere caring.

The only limit to adding value in the selling process is your own creativity. You must make this your goal: to seek, identify, and take action on steps that can transform your contact with the client. You want to move from ritual selling activities to value-added activities that reach beyond your prospect's expectations.

Value must also be added after the prospect is a client. If you add value after the sale has been made, you will ensure client retention, as well as increase your opportunities for generating referrals.

You must continually review your client list and create a plan to add value to each client relationship. If you have built your business on relationships rather than transactions, you have collected enough information to create a value plan for each client.

The best client value plan should be well thought out and unique for each client. For example, if you are familiar with your client's hobbies, a subscription to an appropriate magazine will probably be a welcome gift and also remind him twelve times a year that you care. Tickets to a theater performance or a special sporting event that you know your client will love will add lots of value, exceed your client's expectations, and take you beyond the product or service into a deeper relationship with him.

If you seek to come up with creative ways to add value to your client relationships, you will undoubtedly find them. If you spend your time thinking about your clients and contributing to their lives, they will be thinking of you when an opportunity to refer you arises. The only way to guarantee that your clients will remain loyal to you is to make them love you. Review your client list one by one and create a plan to give each and every one of them some love. You'll eliminate the competition, stand out in a competitive marketplace, and get lots of love back.

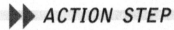 ACTION STEP

SAY THANK YOU IN A BIG WAY

One of the best ways to deliver value in your relationship is to say thank you in a big way. Conduct client appreciation events that will add value to the lives of your clients. There is no limit to the creative yet relatively inexpensive events you can conduct. (Make sure, if applicable in your case, that you are in compliance with National Association of Securities Dealers rules on how much you can spend per person.) Here are a few ideas you might want to consider:

» Golf outings on a premier course
» Symphony orchestra tickets
» Barbecues and picnics
» Cooking lessons with well-known chefs
» Motivational or personal growth seminars
» Birthday, anniversary, and retirement parties
» Spectator sports events
» Dinners at first-class restaurants
» Academy Award party with a big-screen TV
» Spa treatments
» Fashion shows
» Beach party

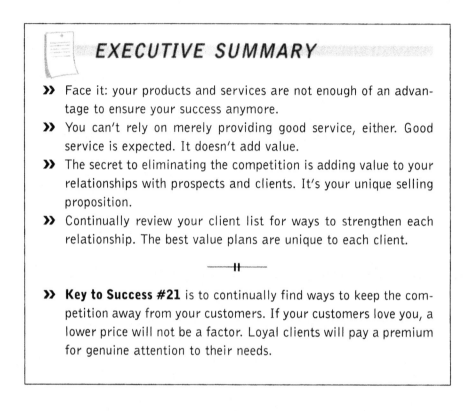

EXECUTIVE SUMMARY

» Face it: your products and services are not enough of an advantage to ensure your success anymore.

» You can't rely on merely providing good service, either. Good service is expected. It doesn't add value.

» The secret to eliminating the competition is adding value to your relationships with prospects and clients. It's your unique selling proposition.

» Continually review your client list for ways to strengthen each relationship. The best value plans are unique to each client.

——ǁ——

» **Key to Success #21** is to continually find ways to keep the competition away from your customers. If your customers love you, a lower price will not be a factor. Loyal clients will pay a premium for genuine attention to their needs.

Energize Your Success

A salesperson, like a storage battery in your car,
is constantly discharging energy. Unless he is recharged
at frequent intervals, he soon runs dry. This is one of
the greatest responsibilities of sales leadership.

—RICHARD GRANT

S ELLING, SUCCESSFULLY EXECUTED, IS A CREATIVE AND SATIS-
fying activity. If you become proficient in the art and science of
selling, your potential for financial success is literally unlimited.

If you decide to seize the opportunity and you are hungry for the
rewards, you must be willing to pay the price in time and energy.
However, it is not uncommon for financial professionals to become
too attached to the rewards and to end up paying a very high price
for them.

The quest for success can result in health problems, failing marriages,
drinking problems, addiction, estranged family relationships, and so on.
The catch-all term for these problems is burnout. Burnout will sabotage
your efforts over the long run. Typically, it is the result of spending too
much energy without taking time to rejuvenate and recuperate. It is usually caused by lack of sleep, poor diet, no exercise, insufficient quiet
time, too few deep emotional connections, lack of spiritual growth, not
enough fun, and working too hard. The symptoms are low energy levels,
minor health problems, lack of motivation, and mediocre performance.

The keys to avoiding burnout are awareness, attention, and action. When you become aware that you are starting to burn out, you must give yourself some attention and take action.

The most powerful system for avoiding or overcoming burnout is entrainment. Entrainment is a principle that was initially discovered by a Dutch scientist named Christian Huygens in 1665. While working on the design of a pendulum clock, Huygens discovered that two pendulums placed near each other, regardless of their size and pattern, would eventually begin swinging at the same rate. The reason has never been discovered, but this synchronization effect is universal. It appears throughout nature and in all the sciences, including chemistry, biology, astronomy, and geology.

When two individual heart muscle cells are brought close together, they begin pulsing in synchrony. This is the classic example of two bodies vibrating in harmony. Another widely observed example of the entrainment effect is the fact that women who live in the same household often find that their menstrual cycles begin to coincide over time.

Similarly, you can maintain balance and health in your life by surrounding yourself with positive energy, the end result you are seeking in your own life. You can entrain life mentally, emotionally, physically, and spiritually. When you become aware of the areas of your life that need to be revitalized or energized, or aspects of your life that need attention, you can entrain yourself in those areas.

However, note that the reverse is also true. Many people are affected by negative entrainment. Unknowingly, in many cases, they entrain with the daily onslaught of negativity in the newspapers and on television. They surround themselves with negative people and spend more time with the problem than with the solution. It is safe to say it is impossible to create success if you entrain with failure.

Two powerful examples of positive entrainment are self-help groups and coaching. The power of these lies not only in the advice you receive but also the revitalization factor. In both cases, you are recharging your energy by surrounding yourself with individuals who have a similar direction and goals.

If there is an area of your life you would like to change or improve, you can probably find and join a group with identical goals or hire a coach who can help you. By spending time with individuals who can provide guidance and support your objectives, you are much more likely to achieve the results you are seeking.

It's interesting that the most successful people have achieved greatness because they practice this principle. All of the best athletes have coaches, most high achievers in sales have had mentors, most great leaders have advisers, and so on. The winners in every field of endeavor realize it is a sign of strength, not weakness, to seek a coach or support group.

—H—

You have the power to maintain your health, life balance, and high performance level by entraining your life in the areas you seek to affect. You must consciously make the best choices in the books you read, the movies you watch, the people with whom you spend your time, and the activities in which you engage. There are an infinite number of positive resources to which you can entrain, and thus revitalize, your life.

Let's look at an example from daily life. One of the most universal problems in the Western world is the difficulty of maintaining an adequate fitness level or target weight, or generally staying in shape. This can be a challenge for people with few goals, and it is even more challenging for people seeking higher levels of success, who have busy and demanding schedules.

If you want to get fit and lose weight, entrain. Join a club or group with a fitness activity you enjoy, such as biking, running, walking, hiking, or swimming. Get a personal trainer. Join a health club. Subscribe to health and fitness magazines. Join a twelve-step program for overeaters. Find partners you can exercise with. Study nutrition. Take cooking classes. Spend lots of time with people who are healthy and fit. Spend time with people who have lost weight and kept it off.

Before you begin to rejuvenate and overcome burnout, however, you must acknowledge the problem. Becoming aware of the problem and how it is affecting you will lead you to the entrainment solution.

In general, seek out people and groups that focus on healing from burnout. Good resources include groups, activities, books, teachers, and coaches. You are also likely to find entrainment solutions for your burnout problem through spas, sports, yoga classes, fitness training, meditation, nature trips, spending more time with your family, a personal trainer, nutritional counseling, and massage. Your personal entrainment formula will be based on your unique needs, problems, and personality. You might have to explore and test to find the right solutions. Remember that your objective is to spend time with people who have what you want.

Entrainment is the solution not only to burnout but also to one of the most common ailments afflicting salespeople: the slump. World-class athletes suffer from it, and so do financial professionals.

You know you are in a slump when your closing ratio is down. As your closing ratio goes down, you are less motivated to make calls and appointments. This leads to less business, which creates an even more pronounced downward spiral. Your confidence gets shaken, which creates yet more problems.

The solution to the slump is to first accept that you are in one. Denial is not just a river in Egypt. It is a roadblock to change and improvement of any kind. Review your closing ratio. If it is dismal, admit to yourself that you are in a slump. Don't worry; it's not the end of the world. It's OK, and you will survive.

If you take the proper action, you will fortify yourself against having as big a slump in the future. And if you do have one, you will have an action plan to effectively get out of it.

The slump usually occurs in conjunction with burnout. Because you are overtired or overworked and your energy is depleted, you no longer have the necessary natural enthusiasm in your presentations. You are phoning it in. You are not totally present for your prospect, and your selling process becomes more mechanical. Because you are not showing up mentally, your ability to connect and to create relationships is severely affected.

These same symptoms can show up when you are doing well. Here, though, the cause is complacency. Because you are doing well, you can fall prey to overconfidence, which results in behaviors similar to burnout. You fail to give it your all, and you do not treat each new opportunity with an equal level of passion.

▶▶ *ACTION STEP*

IF YOU WANT TO FLOWER: BUILD YOUR GREENHOUSE

The underlying strategy for getting out of a selling slump is to build yourself a greenhouse—in other words, create the perfect environment in which to perform at your best. You cannot force yourself out of a slump, and trying to mechanically work your way out of it can be frustrating and counterproductive.

When you apply this greenhouse principle, you put together a variety of elements that allow you to flourish and grow. And as greenhouses can be set up to provide optimal growing conditions for different types of plants, so too must you find the combination of elements that suits you best. Your greenhouse is unique, because you need a special combination of conditions to produce at your best.

Following is a list of elements to consider including in your greenhouse. By incorporating some or all of these, you will begin to create positive energy and momentum in your life, allowing you to come out of your slump and achieve the results you are capable of. This is a list to prime your creative pump. You must explore, experiment, and take some risks. If, on the other hand, you keep doing what you've been doing, there is a good chance you will keep getting what you've been getting.

65 Ways to Snap Out of It

1. Take a vacation
2. Meditate
3. Take an art class
4. Get a personal sales coach
5. Spend lots of time in nature
6. Get rid of your television set
7. Pray
8. Spend time with horses
9. Avoid attempting to sell anything for two weeks
10. Learn a new sport
11. Take a yoga class
12. Ask friends who are successful how they get out of a slump
13. Break as many patterns as possible—do things differently
14. Visualize your positive future twice a day
15. Read your mission statement twice a day
16. Take a fire-walking seminar
17. Get a pet
18. Start therapy
19. End therapy
20. Make a list of the twenty things you love to do, and do them
21. Learn how to play a musical instrument
22. Join a theater group
23. Take singing lessons
24. Rent your favorite funny movies and watch one every night for a month
25. Take a class in creative writing
26. Watch the sunrise
27. Watch the sunset
28. Play your favorite dance music and dance
29. Take dancing lessons
30. Go to a spa and get a massage
31. Make a list of all the things in your life you are grateful for
32. Go for a drive in the country and purposely get lost

33. Spend a day at an aquarium watching the fish swim
34. Buy a book of motivational quotes and read them
35. Spend a day in the critical care unit of a local hospital
36. Call everyone you love and tell them you love them
37. Keep a journal
38. Play more golf
39. Play less golf
40. Go for a walk every day
41. Take a ride in a hot-air balloon
42. Become active in your favorite charity
43. Listen to motivational tapes
44. Keep fresh flowers near you every day
45. Enroll in a personal growth seminar
46. Take sky-diving lessons
47. Give up coffee and alcohol
48. Climb a mountain
49. Take some risks
50. Go camping
51. Go fishing
52. Take a hot bath with candles and incense burning
53. Mentally review all the sales you are most proud of
54. Read inspirational books
55. Twice a week for a month, try working at home
56. Spend lots of time at the beach
57. Become a vegetarian for ninety days
58. Go to a metaphysical bookstore and explore
59. Join a self-help group
60. Lose five pounds
61. Instead of walking, skip everywhere you go
62. Have dinner with your best friend
63. Read anything by Ralph Waldo Emerson
64. Make contact with old friends
65. Renew your marriage vows

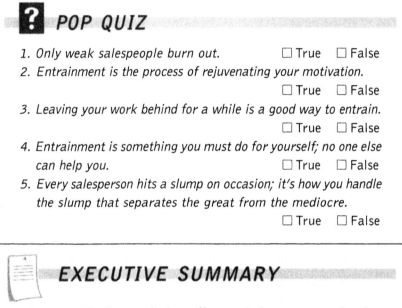

POP QUIZ

1. Only weak salespeople burn out.   ☐ True   ☐ False
2. Entrainment is the process of rejuvenating your motivation.
                                             ☐ True   ☐ False
3. Leaving your work behind for a while is a good way to entrain.
                                             ☐ True   ☐ False
4. Entrainment is something you must do for yourself; no one else
   can help you.   ☐ True   ☐ False
5. Every salesperson hits a slump on occasion; it's how you handle
   the slump that separates the great from the mediocre.
                                             ☐ True   ☐ False

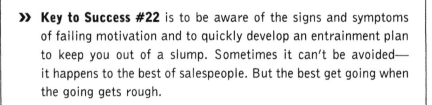

EXECUTIVE SUMMARY

》 Burnout will sabotage the best efforts and often causes a sales slump.

》 The keys to avoiding or overcoming burnout are awareness, attention, and action.

》 Use the entrainment principle. By spending time with people who can guide you and support your objectives, you are much more likely to achieve results.

》 When you apply the "greenhouse principle," you'll create an environment in which you can flourish and break out of your slump.

》 Break old patterns of negativity and introduce positive new elements into your life.

———— ‖ ————

》 Key to Success #22 is to be aware of the signs and symptoms of failing motivation and to quickly develop an entrainment plan to keep you out of a slump. Sometimes it can't be avoided—it happens to the best of salespeople. But the best get going when the going gets rough.

Resources

Prospecting Strategies: How to Create a Steady Stream of Profitable New Business

THERE ARE AN ENDLESS NUMBER of selling strategies and techniques that you can use to generate profitable business opportunities. Your goal should be to zero in on a few strategies that you enjoy using and that work well for you, and then to get into the habit of using them over and over again. (To understand why repeatable activities are important for your business, read Key 8: Develop a Marketing Rhythm.) The following are just a small sampling of the many activities you can use to develop a marketing rhythm. Before you dismiss them as too simplistic, try some of them. They are all proven, highly effective prospecting techniques and have been employed by some of the financial industry's top producers.

Send a Letter with Stuff

You can get lots of attention and an incredibly high appointment ratio if you send a prospecting letter "with stuff"—that is, an interesting object inside. Get a list of people in your target market, such as small business owners or professionals. Ideally, you want a list with at least 100 names. Call each person to confirm the address.

Mail twelve letters on Friday and follow up with a call to each prospect on the following Thursday. For every twelve calls, you can expect to get approximately two appointments. The following week, mail twelve more letters, and follow up in the same way.

Put all the names into your contact management software. For every group of twelve letters you send out, you will need to call back about seven prospects because they weren't in, were busy, or asked to be called back.

After four or five weeks, your "sales funnel" will be filled, and you will have lots of calls to make each week. You will be creating two or three appointments with your target market every week and closing new business.

Below are three sample letters with stuff that get excellent responses and are proven winners. (Be sure to consult your compliance department for approval before using any of these.)

The $2 Bill Letter

Go to the bank and buy 100 new, crisp $2 bills. Mail a prospecting letter with one of these bills attached to twelve people on your list. Here is a sample of a letter you can adapt for your products and services.

Prospect Jones
1111 Prospect Blvd.
Anywhere, USA 33333

Dear Mr. Jones,

This $2 bill gets your attention, doesn't it? That's because it's a little bit different from lots of letters you receive every day.

Our financial solutions are also different and immeasurably more valuable than a $2 bill.

I'd like to spend just twenty minutes with you to show you how our financial strategies can help you (reduce taxes, create financial security, plan for retirement, etc.). I'm confident that after you have seen our concepts and heard our ideas, you will feel your time was well spent.

I'll call you soon to arrange a time that is mutually convenient for us to get together. I look forward to meeting with you.

Sincerely,
Joe Professional

The Little Doggie Letter

Go to a toy store and buy a bunch of cute, furry stuffed dog toys for about $5 each. Mail them with a customized version of the following letter in a third-day FedEx envelope. It doesn't cost much more than the regular mail and will get lots more attention.

Prospect Jones
1111 Prospect Blvd.
Anywhere, USA 33333

Dear Mr. Jones,

Ever wish you had a "dog's life"? You know, where someone feeds you, gives you shelter, scratches behind your ears, and rubs your tummy every time you roll over? Sounds pretty good, right? Well ... I'm not writing to offer those services. But I am trying to get your attention—without "dogging" you—as someone you should meet, someone who can have a very positive impact on your financial future.

What's this all about? I believe I can help you achieve your financial goals, and I can prove it. I specialize in working with (small business owners, seniors, parents with growing families, etc.), showing them how to:
- Increase their after-tax wealth through unique financial strategies
- Decrease their taxes
- Increase their confidence in maximizing their financial objectives

I'll be calling you in the near future to set up a time—thirty minutes, max— where we can meet personally and discuss the work I have done to help other (small business owners, seniors, parents with growing families, etc.) reduce their taxes and increase their after-tax wealth.

Is it worth meeting with me for thirty minutes? I know it's a risk—after all, we have never met. I won't scratch your ears, pat your head, or rub your tummy. But even so, my clients tell me that they enjoy my visits. So, since the risk is small, the time allotment short, and the financial impact potentially great, why not take a chance?

I'll call you in the next few days to schedule a visit. If nothing else, you may at least enjoy my sense of humor. Let's find out.

Sincerely,
Joe Professional

P.S. If you don't come away from the meeting with at least one unique idea, one that has potential for you, I will go away and never return—yes, I mean never! I won't ever dog you for another meeting! Now that is a no-risk promise.

The Block of Wood Letter

Get a Dun and Bradstreet list of companies in your area. This will provide you with the information you need to qualify local companies properly. It will tell you how many employees the company has, its annual sales, what type of company it is, and so on.

You will probably want to target small business owners, since they are one of the most lucrative target markets. They are also one of the most accessible. Small business owners are one of the largest niche markets for affluent households. The Dun and Bradstreet list will provide you with the name of the president who is the person you will be targeting with this technique.

Once you have a solid list of qualified prospects, go to your local lumberyard or home building store. Have them cut a sheet of three-quarter-inch plywood into pieces the size of postcards, approximately four inches by six inches. You can buy it pre-sanded.

Prepare adhesive labels and attach them on one side with your return address and postage. On the back of the block, write, "I have ideas that are stronger than this." Follow up with a phone call to the business and say, "Hi, I'm Joe Professional, I'm the gentleman who sent you a block of wood in the mail."

Harness E-mail for New and Repeat Business Opportunities

E-mail can be one of the most effective systems for attracting qualified prospects and creating repeat business with existing clients. You can send topical information to create raise-your-hand selling opportunities that generate a steady stream of fresh leads.

Using "teaser headline" and well written copy you can generate responses from qualified prospects who are interested in finding out more about the topic or concept in which you are creating interest. You can focus e-mail on various financial issues that your existing clients or new prospects might be interested in.

For example: "You have worked hard and sacrificed much or your life for your business ... Don't you deserve a deferred compensation plan by your company?"

Or "Why risk everything you spent your life working for? You could lose your savings, your business, and your assets. Find out how to protect yourself lawsuits that can devastate you and your family."

Let's assume you have a limited professional relationship with a client. Perhaps you are providing one financial product such as auto or home insurance and you are interested in informing your current clients that you are now offering investment products. E-mail contact will enable you to get the word out to existing clients and expand the relationship.

E-mail also provides one more technique for "touching" your existing clients. You can program e-mail communications to stay in front of your clients effortlessly. Birthday cards, anniversary cards, and New Year's cards will appear on their computers reminding them of your relationship with them.

E-mails can be sent to referrals that have special personalized notes from the referrer regarding the value of your services and quality of your work. You will be notified if and when the referred prospect opened the e-mail you sent.

E-mails can be used to invite clients to seminars and client events. The person who is invited can accept or reject the invitation online. You can manage the statistics online tracking the number of invitations that were sent, when they were sent, and how many accepted invitations.

If you conduct client events such as dinners, golf outings, picnics, and the like, you can take digital pictures of your clients at the event and create a photo album. You'll win lots of friends and create loyalty when you send out the album after the event.

You can send out e-newsletters to your clients five or ten times a year. Every month or two they will receive a customized newsletter that can update your clients on current financial matters. You can also include inspirational or motivational messages in your newsletters to add value to your relationship.

Technology using e-mail to arouse interest in products, create client loyalty, improve retention, and increase cross-selling opportunities is a simple yet powerful strategy to include in your sales and marketing efforts. It requires a minimum investment of time and money and will undoubtedly result in a substantial return.

One of the best resources for e-mail marketing and relationship development is Identity Branding. This company will do everything for you, depending on your needs, for a nominal cost. Contact them at:

Identity Branding
2007 Yanceyville Street, Suite 270
Greensboro, NC 27405
800-851-8169
www.identitybranding.com

Create Strategic Alliances with CPAs

Relationships with CPAs clearly offer incredible referral opportunities for financial professionals. One of the best ways to introduce yourself and your services is to offer CPA continuing education programs and then expand the relationships.

First, identify firms large enough to offer programs on-site during lunchtime. Because you are on-site, it is easy and convenient for CPAs to come, so your program will be well-attended throughout the year, regardless of the season.

Follow up your continuing education programs by offering additional sessions that will help CPAs build or manage their practice more effectively. For example, most CPA firms today are on the lookout for strategies and techniques for marketing their services more effectively.

Most CPAs have practically no sales and marketing skills. Today's competitive marketplace has created pressures for lots of CPAs to become more proactive in this area. After you have initiated relationships with the CPAs, you almost certainly can provide insights on how to generate new business opportunities with referrals, seminars, client events, networking, and community involvement.

If you are conducting financial seminars you might want to invite them to your seminars. Many CPAs are interested in learning more about investments, insurance, and other financial topics. If you develop enough trust and the accountant feels his clients will benefit from your presentation, there might be an opportunity to offer your program to the CPA's clients.

When you are conducting client dinners or client appreciation events of any kind always remember to ask you clients to invite their CPA to the event. There is no more ideal of an environment to initiate a relationship with a CPA than at an event where most of the participants will be expressing positive thoughts and feelings about you. You will find that most CPA firms today are on the lookout for strategies and techniques for marketing their services more effectively.

Continue developing your relationships by taking individuals out to lunch. Stay focused on how you can help them. Allow the relationship to develop naturally, learning about their culture, business model, and challenges.

As was mentioned in Key 18: Cultivate Your Referrals, the most effective way to receive referrals is to give them. If you are continually referring new business opportunities or resources it is only a matter of time before the CPAs you are helping will refer others to you.

Yet keep in mind that your objective is to initiate a long-term relationship, rather than short-term referral business. So above all, you must make it your primary objective to establish trust and make friends. Over time, you will see that lucrative business opportunities begin to evolve with this important group of professionals.

Contact Management Software Programs

THE FOLLOWING SOFTWARE PROGRAMS are available to enable you to automate your sales efforts. These programs will ensure timely contact and follow-up and help you to manage all aspects of your prospect and client relationships. If you're still using the antiquated card box system and are not convinced you need to automate, do yourself a favor and read Key 10: Automate Your Sales Process.

Act4Advisors
Allied Financial Software
800-831-7636
www.Act4Advisors.com

Interactive Advisory Software
IAS
800-821-7355
www.iassoftware.com

Advisors Assistant
Client Marketing Systems, Inc.
800-799-4267
www.climark.com

Gorilla 2.15
The Bill Good Marketing System
800-678-1480
www.billgood.com

Client Data Systems
EZ-Data, Inc.
800-777-9188
www.ez-data.com

Junxure-I
CRM Software, Inc.
866-CRM-Tool
www.GoWithCrm.com

dbcams
FCSI
877-432-2267
www.dbcams.com

ProTracker
ProTracker Software
603-926-8085
www.ProTracker.com

Goldmine
Goldmine Software
800-654-3526
www.goldminesw.com

Credential and Professional Designations Directory

ONE THE MOST EFFECTIVE WAYS to establish yourself as an expert is to obtain the proper credentials. Professional designations position you as an expert and instill confidence in your clients and prospects. Below is a list of recognized designations and contact information for the organizations that confer them.

AAMS

Accredited Asset Management Specialist

Awarded for expertise in investment, insurance, tax, retirement, and estate planning

> College for Financial Planning
> 6161 South Syracuse Way
> Greenwood Village, CO 80111
> 303-220-1200
> www.fp.edu

AEP

Accredited Estate Planner

Awarded by the National Association of Estate Planners & Councils to estate planners, attorneys, and trust officers

> The American College
> 270 South Bryn Mawr Avenue
> Bryn Mawr, PA 19010
> 610-526-1000
> www.amercoll.edu

AFC

Accredited Financial Counselor

Awarded by the Institute for Personal Finance, with an emphasis on technical expertise and ethics

> Accredited Financial Counseling and Education

> 2121 Arlington Avenue
> Upper Arlington, OH 43221
> 614-485-9650
> www.afcpe.org

CDP

Certified Divorce Planner

Awarded for expertise in handling the financial aspects of divorce

> Institute for Certified Divorce Planners
> 6395 Gunpark Drive, Suite W
> Boulder, CO 80301
> 800-875-1790
> www.institutecdp.com

CFA

Chartered Financial Analyst

Awarded to investment advisers, money managers, and securities analysts for expertise in securities analysis

> Association for Investment Management and Research
> P.O. Box 3668
> 560 Ray C. Hunt Drive
> Charlottesville, VA 22903-0668
> 800-247-8132
> www.aimr.org

CFP
Certified Financial Planner
Awarded for financial planning experience and extensive course work
Certified Financial Planner
Board of Standards
1700 Broadway
Denver, CO 80290
303-830-7500
www.cfp-board.org

CFS
Certified Fund Specialist
Awarded for expertise in mutual funds
Institute of Business and Finance
7911 Herschel Avenue, Suite 201
La Jolla, CA 92037-4413
800-848-2029
www.icfs.com

ChFC
Chartered Financial Consultant
Awarded for expertise in financial planning
The American College
270 Bryn Mawr Avenue
Bryn Mawr, PA 19010
610-526-1000
www.amercoll.edu

CIMA
Certified Investment Management Analyst
Awarded for investment management consulting experience
Investment Management Consulting Association
9101 E. Kenyon Avenue, Suite 3000

Denver, CO 80237
303-770-3377
www.imca.org

CIMC
Certified Investment Management Consultant
Awarded to consultants who work with clients and money managers
Institute for Certified Investment Management Consultants
1101 17th Street, N.W.
Washington, D.C. 20036
202-452-8670
www.icimc.org

CLU
Chartered Life Underwriter
Awarded for expertise in insurance
The American College
270 South Bryn Mawr Avenue
Bryn Mawr, PA 19010
610-526-1000
www.amercol.edu

CMFC
Chartered Mutual Fund Counselor
Awarded to financial advisers for expertise in mutual funds
College for Financial Planning
6161 South Syracuse Way
Greenwood Village, CO 80111
303-220-1200
www.fp.edu

CRPC

Chartered Retirement Planning Counselor

Awarded for expertise in retirement planning for individuals

College for Financial Planning
6161 South Syracuse Way
Greenwood Village, CO 80111
303-220-1200
www.fp.edu

CRPS

Chartered Retirement Plans Specialist

Awarded for expertise in retirement plans for businesses and their employees

College for Financial Planning
6161 South Syracuse Way
Greenwood Village, CO 80111
303-220-1200
www.fp.edu

CSA

Certified Senior Advisor

Awarded for expertise in financial issues relevant to seniors

Society of Certified Senior Advisors
1777 S. Bellaire Street, Suite 230
Denver, CO 80222
800-353-1785
www.society-csa.com

CTFA

Certified Trust and Financial Advisor

Awarded for expertise in trusts, tax law, investments, personal finance, and fiduciary responsibilities

Institute for Certified Bankers
American Bankers Association
1120 Connecticut Avenue, N.W.
Washington, DC 20036
800-226-5377
www.aba.com

PFS

Personal Finance Specialist

Awarded to CPAs with financial planning expertise

American Institute of Certified Public Accountants
1211 Avenue of the Americas
New York, NY 10036
212-596-6200
www.aicpa.org

RFC

Registered Financial Consultant

Awarded to licensed insurance and securities professionals

International Association of Registered Financial Consultants
The Financial Planning Building
2507 North Verity Parkway
Middletown, OH 45042
www.iarfc.org

Sample Mission Statements

THE SAMPLE MISSION STATEMENTS BELOW are based on those of practicing financial professionals. Some of them reflect a blend of mission and values. There is no perfect mission statement; what is important is that you have a clear statement of the purpose of your business. To learn more about mission statements, why you should have one, and what impact it will have on your business, read Key 3: Position with Mission.

"Our mission is to continually provide our clients with financial solutions. We are dedicated to building and maintaining relationships based on delivering the highest-quality experience to our clients. All of our advice is given solely to further their best interest."

"Our mission is very simple: to make a significant contribution to the quality of our clients' lives."

"Operating with the highest level of integrity and professionalism, we are dedicated to helping our clients achieve their ultimate financial goals."

"The mission that drives our organization is our clients' peace of mind. We help our clients achieve personal freedom and the ability to live their dreams."

"Our mission is to become a trusted adviser in the lives of our clients. We provide guidance based on uncompromising integrity and world-class personal service."

Sample Smart Questions to Ask Your Prospects

HERE ARE SOME SMART QUESTIONS you can include in your sales conversations. These questions are a way of opening up and deepening the dialog between you and your prospect. They are particularly useful for finding out what is really important to him or her. Include the questions that will work for you, your products and services, and your style. For more tips on listening, questioning, and presenting skills, see Key 14: Master the Art of Communication.

Smart Questions for LIFE PLANNING

If you had all the money you needed, what would you do with your life?

Why is money important to you?

What are the most important goals in your life that you will need to plan for?

What do you need to feel financially secure?

What activities do you see yourself doing in the future?

What future events are you unsure you will be prepared for financially?

Has anyone ever given you a second opinion regarding your financial plan?

What does financial freedom mean to you?

How would you like to be remembered by your family and friends?

Smart Questions for INVESTING

How did you get your money to invest?

What is your asset allocation plan?

What is your investment philosophy?

How have you diversified your investments?

How successful have your investments been?

What kinds of investments have you made in the past?

What is the best financial decision you have ever made?

What have you liked and what have you disliked about your investments?

Have you been using the services of an adviser, or do you prefer to do it yourself?

Are there any companies you would prefer not to invest in for moral reasons?

What are your expectations from me as your adviser?

Smart Questions for FAMILY MATTERS

Who else besides you is affected by your financial decisions?

How much and in what ways do you want to contribute to the lives of your children and leave a legacy to them?

How much and in what ways do you want to contribute to the lives of your grandchildren and leave a legacy to them?

Do your children have their own savings accounts?

Do your children have their own Roth IRAs or UGMA accounts?

Do you have any family members with special needs or disabilities?

How will you want or need to become financially responsible for the well-being and care of your parents?

Smart Questions for BUSINESS OWNERS

What is your succession plan for your business?

What is your exit strategy?

Who will own, control, or run your business when you retire or die?

To what extent will your family be involved in your business in the future?

Which employees are critical to the success and future of your business?

What are your key business concerns?

Smart Questions for RISK MANAGEMENT

How do you feel about life insurance?

What prompted your purchase of life insurance?

How did you calculate your life insurance needs?

How did you select the company or agent you are currently doing business with?

What would motivate you to buy life insurance in the future?

Would you consider buying life insurance on your spouse or children?

How much disability insurance do you have?

What are the maximum monthly benefits, and how long will you receive them?

What have you done to protect your assets against lawsuits from divorce, bankruptcy, your children's creditors, sexual harassment, product liability, and workers' compensation claims?

Smart Questions for *RETIREMENT PLANNING*

Do you have a retirement plan?

What are your retirement dreams?

What is your plan to make your retirement dreams come true?

How much will you need to achieve your retirement dreams?

Is your retirement plan on track?

How much do you have in your retirement plan?

Do you have a plan to withdraw your retirement funds?

Do you completely understand the details of your employer's retirement plan?

Do you know how much you will be receiving from Social Security?

Smart Questions for *ESTATE PLANNING*

Do you have a current will?

In the event that you become incapable of making decisions, do you have a durable power of attorney?

Who are the beneficiaries of your estate?

Who are the guardians of your children?

Who are the trustees of your estate?

How do you plan to pay your estate tax?

What is your favorite charity, religious organization, school, or cause?

Why is this group important to you?

Would you rather give your money to your favorite organization or to Uncle Sam?

Sample Scripts to Make
Your Closing Ratios Soar

THE SCRIPTS SHOWN HERE will help you communicate your message and close more sales. These scripts are examples of how you can craft your words to achieve your objectives and reach your prospects more effectively. Amend, revise, refine, and personalize them for your own delivery style and target market. And don't forget to continue developing your own. If you're wary about using scripts, read Key 20: Close More Sales with Scripting, to learn why they are one of the best tools available to your business.

"The ultimate goal of any investment program is to increase the number of eggs in the basket. Most people are focused on putting more eggs with high returns in their basket. But they forget about the fox that keeps robbing the henhouse. If you fail to protect the henhouse from the fox, soon you won't have many eggs left. Likewise, the annuity I want to show you will protect you from getting robbed by the negative effects of inflation."

"Annuities protect you from the destructive effects of taxation. It's like putting your stocks or mutual funds in a plastic bag. The bag becomes a wrapper that gives your investments tax-sheltered protection."

"The best way to understand the effects of inflation is to look at postage stamps. In 1983, it cost you 20 cents to mail a letter. Today it costs 37 cents. That's an increase of 85 percent. Now imagine how much more it will cost you twenty years from now, when you retire, to pay your electric bill, phone bill, and so on. It's definitely going to cost you lots more. That's why we need to create a plan to effectively deal with this problem."

"Mr. Smith, we make an effort to be different from other people in the investment community. Most advisers spend 80 percent of their time looking for new clients and 20 percent of their time taking care of the ones they have. In my business, I prefer to reverse those numbers and spend 80 percent of my time helping my clients solve their financial problems. To do this, I need your help. My ideal clients are people just like you. Whom do you know who is also a (small business owner, retiree, salesperson, etc.) and would benefit from my services?"

"How much life insurance costs depends on who is paying for it. If the head of the family pays for it, it really costs very little. The relatively few dollars a month paid would doubtless be spent on something temporary, if he or she didn't use that money to buy life insurance.

"But if the family has to pay for the expenses that life insurance would have covered, the costs are far higher, and not only in a financial sense. Not having life insurance can cost children their mother's care, if she is forced to go to work to support them after their father's death.

"Its absence could cost a widow her home, if she is unable to make the mortgage payments on it after her husband passes away.

"Parents who don't have life insurance can later cost their sons or daughters a college education that they badly want and need.

"A lack of life insurance can cost a widow her pride, if she has to accept handouts from her family to supplement her Social Security benefits.

"Not having life insurance can cost the respect of a husband and father who loved his family and provided for them while he was alive but failed to protect them against the loss of his income.

"Buying life insurance is a combination of caring, common sense, character, and love."

"It has been said that if you had the perfect retirement plan, only one check would bounce: the one that was written to pay for the funeral. Unfortunately, nobody can predict how long we are going to live. We do know people are living longer today than they ever have. If you live to be sixty-five without any major illness, there is an excellent chance you will live to be eighty-five. Your job is to keep yourself going, and my job is to help you keep your money going."

About the Authors

Jim Benson is president and chief executive officer of Clark Benson, LLC. Prior to joining Clark Benson, he served as president and chief executive officer of John Hancock Life Insurance Company. Before assuming that role, he was president of John Hancock Sales and Marketing, overseeing the individual life, annuity, and long-term care businesses. Prior to joining John Hancock Financial Services, he was president of MetLife's Individual Business unit, responsible for MetLife Financial Services, New England Financial, GenAmerica Financial, MetLife Investors Group, and Nathan & Lewis Securities. He also was chairman and CEO of Boston-based New England Financial, as well as chairman and CEO of GenAmerica Financial Corporation, both MetLife affiliates. Before joining New England Financial and MetLife in 1997, Mr. Benson held the dual position of president and CEO of Equitable Companies, Inc., and was CEO of its flagship life insurance operation, Equitable Life Assurance Society. Prior to joining The Equitable in 1993, he was president of the New York office of Management Compensation Group, an insurance brokerage and executive benefits consulting firm. From 1968 to 1984, he held a variety of positions in sales, marketing, and product development with Pacific Mutual Life Insurance Company.

Mr. Benson graduated from the University of Illinois with a B.A. in Economics and earned an M.B.A. from the University of Southern California. He holds a CLU designation. Mr. Benson serves on the boards of the United Way of Massachusetts Bay, Achilles Track Club, Hospital for Special Surgery, Bryant College, and the University of Illinois. He also serves on the Visiting Committee to the Harvard University Graduate School of Education and the Harvard University Resource Committee. In addition, he is founder and chairman of World T.E.A.M. Sports, an organization dedicated to providing opportunities through sports for people with disabilities.

Paul Karasik is the president of The Business Institute, a sales and management training and consulting company. He has devoted eighteen years to helping America's financial industry professionals achieve their goals.

Mr. Karasik is the author of four business classics, *Sweet Persuasion* and *Sweet Persuasion For Managers,* published by Simon and Schuster; *How To Make It Big In The Seminar Business,* published by McGraw-Hill; and *Seminar Selling: The Ultimate Resource Guide for Marketing Financial Services,* published by Irwin Professional Publishing. His most recent books include *Mastering the Art of Wholesaling, How to Market to High-Net-Worth Households,* and *Brilliant Thoughts.*

He is a monthly columnist for *On Wall Street* magazine and is regularly featured in leading financial industry publications including *Investment Adviser, CFP Today, Registered Rep, National Underwriter,* and *Bank Investment Marketing.*

Mr. Karasik is the founder of the American Seminar Leaders Association and a popular presenter at professional conferences and seminars throughout North America.

About Bloomberg

Bloomberg L.P., founded in 1981, is a global information services, news, and media company. Headquartered in New York, the company has sales and news operations worldwide.

Bloomberg, serving customers on six continents, holds a unique position within the financial services industry by providing an unparalleled range of features in a single package known as the BLOOMBERG PROFESSIONAL® service. By addressing the demand for investment performance and efficiency through an exceptional combination of information, analytic, electronic trading, and Straight Through Processing tools, Bloomberg has built a worldwide customer base of corporations, issuers, financial intermediaries, and institutional investors.

BLOOMBERG NEWS®, founded in 1990, provides stories and columns on business, general news, politics, and sports to leading newspapers and magazines throughout the world. BLOOMBERG TELEVISION®, a 24-hour business and financial news network, is produced and distributed globally in seven languages. BLOOMBERG RADIO^{SM} is an international radio network anchored by flagship station BLOOMBERG® 1130 (WBBR-AM) in New York.

In addition to the BLOOMBERG PRESS® line of books, Bloomberg publishes *BLOOMBERG MARKETS®* magazine. To learn more about Bloomberg, call a sales representative at:

London:	+44-20-7330-7500
New York:	+1-212-318-2000
Tokyo:	+81-3-3201-8900

FOR IN-DEPTH MARKET INFORMATION and news, visit the Bloomberg website at **www.bloomberg.com,** which draws from the news and power of the BLOOMBERG PROFESSIONAL® service and Bloomberg's host of media products to provide high-quality news and information in multiple languages on stocks, bonds, currencies, and commodities.